# The
# Management
## — *of* —
# MENTORING

# The
# Management
## *of*
# MENTORING

## policy issues

EDITED BY
**DEREK GLOVER AND GEORGE MARDLE**

**KOGAN
PAGE**

London • Philadelphia

First published in 1995

Kogan Page Limited
120 Pentonville Road
London N1 9JN

© Derek Glover, George Mardle and named contributors, 1995

**British Library Cataloguing in Publication Data**

A CIP record for this book is available from the British Library.

ISBN 0 7494 1598 3

Typeset by Saxon Graphics Ltd, Derby
Printed and Bound in Great Britain by Biddles Ltd, Guildford and Kings Lynn

# Contents

# Contributors

## Editors

**Derek Glover**, Research Associate, Department of Education, The University of Keele, was formerly head of Burford School and Community College, Oxfordshire. He took early retirement in order to complete a PhD in school community relationships, and has subsequently undertaken teaching and research work with Keele, Leicester and The Open universities. He has published work on school organization, financial management and the management of reputation, and coordinated the field work for this research.

**George Mardle**, Lecturer, Department of Education, The University of Keele, is responsible for the further education and policy elements of the PGCE course. He also manages the MA course and supervises PhD students in policy development, multicultural and women's issues. He is a county councillor and chairman of Staffordshire Social Services committee. He has published work on community education development, political education and current developments in FE. He has directed the Esmee Fairbairn research at Keele University.

## Esmee Fairbairn Research Team

**Tricia Evans** is lecturer in English in Education, The University of Keele. She was formerly head of faculty in a large comprehensive school, and is currently director of the secondary undergraduate education course. She has published books on the teaching of English and drama in secondary and primary schools.

**Gerry Gough** was formerly a headteacher. He is a member of the Keele Successful Schools Project, statistician for the Keele research programme and PGCE education tutor.

**Michael Johnson** is Director of the Two Towns Project, The University of Keele. He was formerly a deputy head in a large comprehensive school, and subsequently a member of the Keele Successful Schools Project, PGCE education and professional studies tutor.

**Mervyn Taylor** is Director, PGCE, at The University of Keele. He has been involved in the development of a partnership scheme for the past three years. He has also been responsible for the links between the university and the Peto Institute, developing appropriate teacher training for those working in conductive education.

The team has been immensely strengthened by five mentors from local Staffordshire and Cheshire schools who have undertaken case study preparation – **Linda Devlin, Dereth Carr, Helen Sharp, Bob Sharpe** and **Richard Siddley.** They have each prepared a report on work within the school in which they work and a contrasted school.

The team has also been helped by the staff of schools and the education departments at Worcester College of Higher Education and St Martins, Lancaster. Their willingness to contribute to the field work is much appreciated, as is the help given by the 20 schools who allowed us to work with them, the 500 associate teachers who gave us their views of their experiences, and the 100 mentors within the Keele partnership of schools.

We are also conscious of the support from the five other university departments of education who have been our partners in the Esmee Fairbairn Mentoring Research Project and with whom we have discussed progress and tested ideas.

# Introduction

Mentoring as a means of teacher education is not a new concept. During the past decade it has enhanced the supervision of students in training by ensuring a continuing relationship with one member of staff in the school, or schools, within which professional training is taking place. The mentor usually becomes responsible for the management of most of the teaching experience for the student as he or she passes through the stages of induction into the school and into teaching, develops competences in class and subject management, and then develops the responsibility and judgement associated with professional maturity. The purpose of this book is to consider the internal and external policy issues that are becoming evident as the changes in initial teacher education (ITE) promulgated in outline by the Department for Education (DfE, 1992) are embedded in practice. Changed approaches are affecting schools, higher education institution departments of initial teacher training (HEIs), and the education system as a totality. Experience shows successful mentors to be teachers who have a clear understanding of the contribution that theory and practice make to subject and teaching development, and who are provided with supportive conditions for their training role.

Nomenclature varies from partnership to partnership but in the subsequent discussions we shall refer to HEI-based staff as 'tutors', to school-based staff as 'mentors', and to students as 'associates' rather than associate teachers or ATs. In general, the partnership between HEIs and schools has been negotiated by the course director and individual heads, often after much local negotiation with teachers' professional associations. The organization of the integration of associates into schools and the focus of administration, with or without some professional teaching role, is the responsibility of a professional mentor in the schools working with a link or professional tutor in the HEI. The development of teaching competences within a subject framework is the responsibility of the subject mentor who liaises with a curriculum tutor in the same subject in the HEI, either directly or through the professional mentor.

The purpose of the Keele University Department of Education investigations has been to ascertain the impact of the shift of a greater proportion of the responsibility for teacher education into the schools. Over the past five years the university has been forging new links and establishing a partnership with the staff of over 30 local schools. There has been a full evaluation of the postgraduate associate experience in both 1993 and 1994. In late 1993 it became clear from discussions with the staff of the schools that mentoring, while frequently very successful as a means of teacher education, was not without its problems and that both the HEI and school staff in the partnership were anxious to chart the strengths and weaknesses of existing arrangements. Research based upon the views of mentors gathered from questionnaires, and a full study of the organization of mentoring in 20 case study schools undertaken by five mentors and a field worker, was accepted for support as part of a six-university scheme funded by the Esmee Fairbairn Charitable Trust. Our research approach is discussed in further detail in the Appendix.

The data obtained from the investigations have been used as the basis for this book. Chapter 1 examines the external influences upon mentoring. These have developed within the context of governmental policy alongside more participative approaches emerging from reconsideration of teacher education by the staff of HEIs. Overall, it seems that both government and profession are working towards a system that places real experience at the heart of teacher education. The practicalities of the organization of this scheme within the schools are examined in Chapter 2, which is concerned with those factors that appear to affect the internal environment for associates. The basic contention here is that there is a tendency for associate experience to be more successful where mentoring is seen by the staff of a school to be a worthwhile activity and where initial teacher training (ITE) is seen as part of a total provision of staff development.

The four case studies in Chapter 3 are offered as examples of the varying organizational frameworks and attempt to show how associates are affected by multiple influences within the schools. The importance of the recruitment, training and professional development of subject mentors and the role of the professional mentor in securing a worthwhile experience are discussed in Chapters 4 and 5. However, mentors and professional mentors are not working in isolation, and the perceived impact of governmental policy on the organization, funding and maintenance of school and HEI partnerships is considered in Chapter 6. This is also concerned with the varying experience gained by associates, an issue that is set into its departmental perspective in Chapter 7, which illustrates the requirements for fostering successful practice in securing departmental as well as individual associate development.

The issue of interaction between the stakeholders is further developed in Chapter 8, which considers the way in which varying mentor, departmental and whole school staff attitudes contribute to associate experience and to the promotion of a mentoring culture within schools. The use of an audit of the mentoring experience is suggested as the basis of quality provision. However, there are limitations to the successful development of schemes in meeting the future needs for teacher education within the schools, and the final chapter suggests how the research work has indicated a way forward in policy planning.

Throughout this book, reference is made to those schools that have given us so much help in undertaking this research. All names used are fictitious and we must stress that the names we have used do not reflect any school that might, by coincidence, have a similar title. We do not think that detective work can yield the identity of the exemplar case study schools, but neither the staff nor associates were unwilling to discuss the issues with us – identification might well have detracted from the open nature of our investigation.

## Reference

Department for Education, 1992 *Initial Teacher Training (Secondary Phase)*, Circular 9/92, London: DfE.

# Chapter 1

# The Policy Context

## George Mardle

The aim of this chapter is to outline the broad policy in which the development of the mentoring framework in teacher education has taken place, and to set our investigation within that context. It will seek to address the macro social, economic and political influences that have promoted the creative turbulence for both higher education institutions and schools in this area. Also addressed will be the policy frameworks within which schools themselves are approaching the questions of mentoring. It will argue that the often crude and narrow assumptions made by government, and which are being challenged by current practice, may themselves provide the basis for future developments in teacher education. They could, if grasped appropriately, promote a model of professionalism that could lead to greater optimism in the development of teacher education.

## The Political Agenda

Clearly, given the limits of the field of investigation within this book, we cannot deal with all of the complex historical roots that might have influenced the education system in general and more specifically teacher education. Nevertheless, it would also be foolish to deny that many of the current themes in the area are not new and reflect contradictions and dilemmas that have been around in the area since the 1870s. As Bolton (1994) argues: 'The general drift of government policy is clear: namely to break up the more or less monolithic pattern of ITT and to decouple it from higher education.' Suffice it to say that this movement of teacher education to the top of the political agenda could be the final part of a plan to implement Tory party thinking on education, which has been a prominent theme in the political arena since the general election of 1979.

Yet to assume that the system has merely been reactive to these circumstances would be to ignore the fact that teacher educators have also been proactive in continually addressing the issues and dilemmas that they have been presented with by government policy. Attempts to recognize good practice and to promote the professional development of reflexive practitioners have not been ignored. Difficulties have arisen because of the lack of dialogue and consultation that seems to have been the hallmark of the government approach in most of its policy formulations, particularly in education.

It will be my concern to argue that while we cannot ignore the dominance of a particular ideological agenda in the changes of the past few years, we nevertheless have a clear duty to future generations to make sure that we promote a highly committed and professional workforce through the development of a thoroughly coherent model of teacher education. This should be one that addresses both the context of what the education and training should be about and an understanding of the balance concerning where it should take place.

It might well be argued, as numerous commentators do (see Centre for Contemporary Cultural Studies, 1981), that the starting point for the creative turmoil that has affected the education system for the past 20 years was the famous Ruskin College speech by Jim Callaghan in 1976, which addressed what he saw as the failings of the then current education system. The agenda that he set, particularly in relation to the centralization and control of the system, was immediately taken up by an incoming Tory government led by Margaret Thatcher, who set about systematically dismantling the careful partnerships of the previous 35 years in a crusade of ideological fervour to win back the 'school system' to traditional values. Backed up by thinkers who wished to finally dispense with 'socialism' in all its forms, particularly in relation to education, it produced a heady cocktail of reform. Many of the proponents could trace their intellectual origins back to the Black Papers in Education (Cox and Boyson, 1970; Cox and Dyson, 1977). They saw as their essential remit the necessity to challenge the progressive hegemony that had been at the forefront of educational thinking, in their opinion, since the 1960s. Standards were too low, old values were being eroded and authority was being challenged. The imagery of traditional classrooms with gentlemen scholars at the front abounded, and was part of the implicit vision throughout the 1980s and into the 1990s in teacher education reform.

However, in challenging the perceived dominance of what Kogan (1978) calls 'insider groups', the politicians in power realized that their agenda for change could not be achieved instantaneously. Not only did England and Wales have one of the most devolved systems of education in the world, but any form of structural change is notoriously difficult to undertake, as McPherson and Raab (1988) argue: 'To focus on changes which formal policies seek is to disregard the fundamental inertia to which all formal policy changes are marginal.'

The policy makers therefore needed to adopt a number of strategies that would allow the new radical agenda to take root. The first was to promote and sustain some kind of moral outrage at the way standards had fallen. Following in the footsteps of the Black Paper rhetoric, the key 'folk devil' to attack was the prevalence of so-called progressive teaching methods. This was linked to a concern about the standards of education achieved in our schools in relation to our international rivals. Meeting these criticisms would essentially destroy the mythology of the comprehensive ideal and set a commonsense approach to the issues of change, particularly in the area of teacher education (Moore, 1994). An ideological void was filled quickly by TINA (There Is No Alternative) arguments such as a 'return to family values' (Margaret Thatcher) and the campaign for 'back to basics' (John Major). The second move was to gradually gain control of the system in order to promote and sustain these particular ideologies. The mechanism used to achieve this was the gradual promotion of the double aims of centralization and marketization. In essence, the state would, through a process of centralization, take control of what was taught in the institutions. This would ensure that the Tory agenda on standards would be achieved. The use of the market in the running of the system would then ensure that this process was achieved in the most efficient and economical way. It would essentially also placate the pressure groups from the two wings of the Tory party, ie, the One Nation Tories and the New Right Liberal Economics wing.

The other important element in the achievement of this change was inherent in the administration of the system. As the politicians saw it, all was not well in relation to state control. Essentially, too many years of corporatist involvement had left the power in the hands of the professionals. However, it was not possible to dismantle this perceived élite all at once. The three central areas of concern were, first, the running of schools where many were under the potentially 'bad' influence of left-wing local authorities; second, the nature of the curriculum, which was seen as diverse and lacking relevance, and also under the possibly 'dangerous' influence of progressive teachers who questioned societal norms; and third, and for our purposes the most important, the control of teacher education itself and the development of future generations of teachers were seen as fundamental to the achievement of an improved education service.

A detailed catalogue of legislation in the 1980s would suggest that basic priorities were always linked around the control of the first two concerns, with the promotion of local management of schools and the gradual erosion of the role of local authorities, coupled with the development of the National Curriculum. There were, however, ominous signs that teacher education was also to be an area for review, with some interesting preliminary skirmishes as evidenced in the Teacher Quality Paper (DfE, 1983), Circular 3/84 (DfE, 1984), and the development of the Council for the Accreditation of Teacher Education (CATE). Nevertheless, it was always on the agenda that teacher education would at some stage become a focus of attention for ministers eager to make their mark or to show purity of commitment with the educational policy gurus from the various right-wing think tanks.

From the early 1990s the main target became the area of teacher education, the alleged last bastion of progressivism and woolly liberal thinking in education. Cleverly, the way in which the debate was orchestrated shows teacher educators as a minority whose only interest is to challenge the common sense orthodoxy (Moore, 1994) which is at the heart of Tory thinking. In summary, the view is that if we can all see the way the education system fails, then we can all see how it is perpetuated if new teachers learn the wrong things; hence we can all see that the best solution to the problem would be to take the education and training of teachers away from the people who promote this theoretical and, to some, dangerous, heresy.

This attack on the teacher educators is therefore the last element in the achievement of an overall educational policy. The view is that if the monopoly of teacher educators can be broken and their opportunity for ideological input minimized, there will be a unified system where teachers know what to teach, through the National Curriculum; how to teach it effectively, through on-the-job training, and in the most efficient manner, through the local management of schools. Neither the simplicity of this argument nor the vitriol with which some politicians describe the role of teacher educators should be underestimated. In a lecture to the Conservative Political Centre in 1993, the then Secretary of State for Education, John Patten, explained: '...we are ensuring that teacher training is precisely that, training – undertaken as much as possible in the school – and not wasted studying dated and irrelevant texts on theory'. More recently, in a debate on the 1994 Education Bill (which incidentally set up the Teacher Training Agency), Rhodes Boyson was heard to state: 'I sometimes think that training for teachers...is a restrictive lower-middle-class practice...people should not be brought in from universities...'.

Yet as many other writers have indicated, the debate which is at the heart of these statements is not new. There has and always will be a debate about the relationship, as in any other practical profession, between theory and practice. What is at issue is the extreme position taken by government and an inability to see that the logical extension of such action might lead to the very point where some of the demands for professional competence cannot be met because their rationale is not understood by classroom practitioners.

## Contemporary Teacher Education

It is helpful at this stage to remind ourselves of the position of teacher education in the latter part of the 20th century. In essence, we have reached a stage where all teachers have a clear professional education and training experience before they are able to practise. While no one would be complacent about the universal achievement of the highest standards in both of these elements, they are nevertheless tried and tested through two models. The first is the professional training model (PGCE). Here the emphasis is on the acceptance of a knowledge base, through an appropriate subject-based degree, with the general input of educational technique and theory as a bolt-on process. The second is that of a concurrent professional training. Here the emphasis is on the development of educational practice and theory alongside that of the necessary subject specialisms. Alternatives have been suggested (sandwich courses, two-year PGCE) but in the world of scarce resources, these two models remain clearly the most viable.

While there has been no clear empirical evidence that either method of training was inadequate and, indeed, reports by Her Majesty's

Inspectorate were generally favourable, the populist stance of the government on teacher quality had to be addressed. Bolton (1994) summarized the situation thus: '... the teaching profession generally, and primary teachers in particular, had been seduced away from sound traditional teaching methods into progressive, soft-centred relativism by academic teacher trainers and various assorted gurus'.

The answer to this criticism from external commentators was to suggest reversion to a much older and more traditional model which, though essentially now disregarded by the professionals, provided the politicians with just the right populist format. What in essence was being suggested was the development, albeit in various guises, of the apprenticeship model. Notable for its simplicity, the basis of this is to provide training for teachers by placing them alongside experts, taking in what is regarded as common sense knowledge of what everyone knows about teaching. It is as if by osmosis students learn by observation and then go into the classroom to repeat what has been seen. This provides implicit socialization into the basic mechanisms of teaching by providing clear and uninterrupted experience of all that is best in practice, without any real interference from discussion based on reflection on context or practice, or from irrelevant theory.

This priority of placing practice at the forefront of the agenda was further supported by the heavy emphasis from the mid-1980s, spurred on by the development of National Vocational Qualifications, on the notion of a system of teaching competences. By moving to an output model rather than a process one, it is clear that the nature of inputs becomes secondary to the real business at hand, which is to provide evidence of accomplishment in the practical situation. However this may be achieved, or whatever inputs are necessary to promote it, as long as it is recorded, we have a clear profile of a potentially skilled technician. Such arguments therefore represent a very succinct and fundamental change in the external understanding of what teaching is about. Is it on the one hand a basically technical accomplishment or, on the other, a reflective and developing professional practice? To put it crudely, are teachers technicians or professionals?

More importantly for a government committed to a moral crusade to reassert the fundamental cultural values of our society, such a model also shifts emphasis onto the moral calibre of the teachers themselves. If teacher educators are to have no real input into the process, then the influence of those who it is assumed are opposed to the revisionist policies of the government is finally diminished. Standards, behaviour and morality come to the fore and, in effect, as Bolton (1994) argues: '...the debate about teacher training has become a debate about fundamental values implicit in, and transmitted by, teachers and schools'.

These arguments about the nature of teacher education are not new, neither is the argument which seems to be at the heart of the discussion, namely the relationship between theory and practice. Clearly any form of education and training for teachers will have a value structure surrounding it, either explicitly or implicitly. Common sense is also a value structure. Furthermore, as indicated previously, there have always been discrepancies between the theory and practice of teacher education (Mardle and Walker, 1980). Centrally, the issue is how best to integrate the three components of prior socialization, theoretical input and on-the-job training to promote the best possible professional development which allows values to be addressed in their context, and not with some implicit ideological prescription.

We might also ask why the emphasis on this prescriptive apprenticeship model has so readily come to the fore. Importantly, the choice of models is not based on simple expediency. If we refer back to the two key elements identified earlier we know that marketization and centralization provide clear messages regarding the government's view of how the education service should develop. There are, therefore, two other important strands of argument which are relevant. First, major changes in the management of schools have led to a clearly managerialist approach to their internal organization. A consequence of this process is to indicate, by a series of control mechanisms, the de-skilling of the teaching profession. So we have a link between a move to change the nature of the teaching activity itself and a clear promotion of an implicit technician model of training. To have provided a professional development model is something which would have been seen as anathema to the underlying values promoted by the government. Second, one of the most important driving forces for change in the public sector has been in the economic sphere. Value for money arguments have always shown the education and training process for teachers to be relatively expensive. The government, by transferring the process away from higher education towards the school system, has been able to meet two aims. In essence it is taking the control of teacher education away from the dominance of the liberal intelligentsia while at the same time promoting developments in institutions basically starved of finance. As with most new innovations in the public sector, there is only recycling of old cash and not development of new.

It might well be argued that mentoring was a clear move by HEIs to counter many of the simplified and philistine approaches which had been trailed by right-wing think tanks throughout the 1980s. It would be wrong, however, to assume that the move was merely a knee-jerk reaction. The idea that there is a major and fundamentally flawed disjuncture between theory and practice in teacher education is yet again part of a useful myth exuded by politicians with a particular agenda to push. The relationship between theory and practice has always promoted a healthy and lively debate. There has been an involvement of schools and teachers in the process of teacher training since the Elizabethan grammar schools. However, what has often happened since 1944 is that in many ways schools were part of the sub-text, a necessary place to go to undertake the practical element, with teachers, but not as the key aspect of the training process. Perhaps that itself led to clear antagonism at times between the higher education input, the school input and the student in training. The old adage of students being told to ignore the 'airy fairy theory' they had learnt in college and concentrate on the real world when they enter teaching practice, is part of the mythology of teacher training courses. Repeatedly, research had traditionally indicated that: '...colleges and university departments deal in theoretical ideals and liberal philosophies which are impractical and irrelevant to the job of teaching. This is facilitated by the "distance" between training institutions and schools' (Mardle and Walker, 1980).

Notwithstanding the general criticism of that general assertion, it has continually provided ammunition for those who wish to attack the inputs of the HEIs. Well before the intention to mount a full attack on teacher education in the 1994 Education Act was evident, the problem was being addressed. Many institutions throughout the 1980s were beginning to challenge these crude notions and work out new methods of links and partnerships between on- and off-the-job education and training. As documented by Wilkin (1990), the idea of partnership between schools and higher education institutions has become the recognized norm of operation and development in the field. Important for our concerns, and central to that development, is the concept of mentoring.

## The Movement Towards Mentoring

The interesting point about the movement towards the use of partner-ship and mentoring in teacher education is that it actually questions the mechanisms by which the debate had been set up and some of the crude responses from politicians that were being promoted. For while at one extreme we might have the notion of learning teaching skills by some kind of osmosis, and at the other a wholly theoretical model of the process, mentoring provides a clearer need to define the role inputs which those involved have to make in the process. What therefore becomes fundamental to the development of partnership arrangements is the way in which the partners involved determine the necessary inputs to teacher education they should make; and how they outline the perceived roles of the participants and the way in which the institutions involved might develop and promote policies which will facilitate such a process.

Mentoring, if we look at other professional groups, is not a new phenomenon. The early developments in this area were in the medical profession, and the internship pattern was drawn upon in pioneering developments in teacher education. However, the differing structural relationship between schools and higher education institutions compared to that in hospitals and medical schools has given rise to a somewhat different emphasis in the developing patterns. It is also clear that education students work from a more diverse and disputed set of foundations of knowledge and experience. Whatever the origins, it is clear that many successful and quite highly developed programmes existed well before the clear national imperative demanded in Circular 9/92 (DfE, 1992).

Early attempts at mentoring were undertaken across a range of insti-tutions. Immediately, the nature of the policy to be adopted and other strategic management issues came to the fore in a debate which contin-ues. There is, for instance, a whole series of professional dilemmas regarding the nature of inputs and the role of the participants. Furthermore, there is a series of individual and structural parameters upon development which have their historical roots in the assumed roles of the participants and which may well conflict with current pres-sures on both schools and higher education institutions caused by the marketization of their work. The basis of good, sound education and training of teachers for the next century will be the way in which participating institutions address these issues.

The fundamental question concerns the roles which ought to be adopted by the HEI and the school in a new partnership. The answer to this dual tension will determine policy development, but is being worked through in a pragmatic rather than theoretical way. Indeed, the very term 'partnership' is potentially fraught with difficulty, given that the necessary democratic processes of discussion and decision making often take time to develop. Furthermore, they can be particularly time-consuming in situations where responses may necessarily require quick decisions while the normal life of the institution has to be maintained. If we add to this the relative autonomy that the institutions and individuals have traditionally valued in their work, we can see the emergence of complex responses as partnerships develop. It is no wonder that even within partnerships there will be a whole range of different responses. Importantly, the development of roles will also need to take into account the current climate of structural turbulence. Schools and higher education institutions have been under enormous pressures since the 1980s to deliver quality and standards across a range of areas. It is an interesting assumption, and one never really empirically investigated to any great extent, that schools do actually want to undertake the major role in teacher education or that teachers see clear advantages in undertaking the role of mentors. It is equally important to investigate the financial parameters within which the whole process is being driven. Market forces and financial constraints do focus the mind. The question is, do they enhance the development of appropriate education and training models for future teachers?

## Interaction

Promotion of policy in the area of practice, I would suggest, is very much a symbiosis of five important factors:

- the response of the higher education institution
- the response of teachers and administrators in the schools
- the organizational responses of the schools
- the cultural responses of the schools
- the interpretation made by the participants of the ideological and economic climate within which they are working.

What is interesting about the interaction of this set of relationships and the way they are to be worked out is that government has not prescribed what exactly should happen. At one level, this could be seen as promoting a clear view of professional independence. At another, it could well be argued that this suggests a tension in the body politic over their precise views of what exactly they want. Importantly, the politicians remain unclear about what exactly the relationship should be because, in the rush to take control of the system, they have not been prepared to wait for pilot schemes to be promoted, developed and evaluated. Perhaps more to the point, in the ever-present search for the goal of value for money, they wish to see the competitive bidding process take its course.

Change, as demonstrated by the administration of all elements of recent educational strategy, takes finance and resources. It has been clear from the mid-1980s that this government has no real intention of providing adequate additional finance for innovation and change, but seeks development through the diversion of existing resources. By leaving the precise details vague then, under the guise of supposed autonomy, the responses should promote some degree of competition between the agencies involved. One only has to see the wide divergence in the transfer of money to schools inherent in policy following Circular 9/92 (DfE, 1992) to see the logic of this process. In such a climate, the pressures and tensions of trying to address the problems of teacher education at institutional level become an important area of investigation and research. Indeed, the whole basis of Keele's research in the area of mentoring has been to investigate the variables in the implementation of this equation.

Developments of policy by individual schools might be analysed in two distinct ways. First, in the way in which the institutional and organizational frameworks which support mentoring develop and, second, in the way in which individual teachers, particularly those who wish to be involved in the mentoring process, see their roles within those frameworks. Thus while most HEIs might be seen as setting most of the agenda initially, it is the response of institutions and individuals which will define the way their roles and responsibilities eventually become embedded within the total process of teacher education. As indicated previously, policy making has started from the assumption that those involved in the management of schools and classroom teachers do actually wish to undertake a major element of the teacher education and training. Indeed, there is some indication from our research that particular individuals and schools are showing some resistance to what they see as another potential imposition by government on their work-load. However, in the context of market forces, local management of schools and cash-starved budgets, many will find the offer of extra resources irresistible, and involvement without proper thought and preparation may be detrimental to school and associates. These attitudes are illustrated in some of the case study and mentor comments: 'The management think that this is just like running a club at the end of the day'; 'The job is unpaid, has no perks, and therefore we can only assume it is seen of little value by the senior management team except as a source of money'; 'I appreciate that this is a politically contentious issue and I deplore any attempt to educate would-be teachers on the cheap'.

For schools, the important question then becomes one of determining the appropriate culture and organization for successful education. The development of mentoring, at least on rational grounds, can easily be justified. It locates practical training in the right arena. It can contribute to the professional development of the teachers involved. It promotes present and future good professional practice. However, justification is not the same as implementation and what becomes important is how far the new models of mentoring become central to the work of the school. For instance, our discussions point to the inclusion of the following issues in the evolution of the partnership:

- How much time will be allocated for the full development of the relationship between mentor and student?
- What transfer of resources from other important elements of the school's work will take place?
- Do the staff of the school or college recognize the processes involved and are they able to change communication and management structures to facilitate the work?
- How does the overall professional development plan of the school promote good practice in the area?
- How is the process to be made to work so that it minimizes the potential for disruption to the pupils?

But the list of practical considerations is endless, and responses are dependent upon institutional culture, personal experience and the organizational context of participating schools and HEIs. Yet, unless schools respond to the philosophical challenges and address the policy

implications of these questions, the whole impetus for change will stag-
nate, frustrations may build up and failure will feed the thinking of
those who may wish to demonstrate failure. This can only result in the
introduction of a more pernicious model which ignores partnership.

## The Research Rationale

No matter how far the school 'sells' the development of mentoring or is
committed to its development through the facilitation of structures, the
ultimate success or failure of mentoring will depend on the involvement
of teachers. Again, our research evidence demonstrates a spectrum of
opinion. Responses by individuals are clearly variable and can have
both negative and positive connotations as outlined in Chapter 8
(Glover *et al.*, 1994). In the present climate of school development
plans, mission statements and the enormous pressure which seems to be
being placed on teachers, the idea of having to respond to mentoring
might be seen as another impossible burden for individuals to shoulder.
Alternatively, if the positive advantages are detailed, it can be seen as a
way towards the clear enhancement of the professional status of the
classroom practitioner. We might legitimately ask who actually becomes
a mentor and why? How is the role defined, who does the defining and
do individuals need special training to do it? Importantly, how does it,
amongst all the other potential avenues available, fit in with a career
profile for the individual? In total, what in effect motivated teachers to
become involved in the mentoring process?

The final area of consideration, and one which links to the wider
ideology of the system, is that of control. Importantly, as we move to a
system of partnership, the mechanisms of training, monitoring, control
over quality and the financial arrangements themselves begin to
change. It remains unclear, for instance, who is accountable to whom
for the mentoring that goes on in schools. Who, for example, would
take the responsibility for a poor mentor – the school or the HEI in the
partnership?

All these policy questions have to be addressed if we are to realize the
full potential of mentoring as an important and fundamental part of
teacher education and training in the future. If we are to challenge
some of the more extreme macro policy arguments detailed earlier,
then partnerships must not only come to terms with the practical

implementation outlined, but also address the more fundamental and ideologically inspired policy initiatives mentioned at the beginning of this chapter. More importantly perhaps, partnerships already need to address the skills, expectations and requirements of teachers working in the 21st century. It seems quite nonsensical that when expectations rise, a government should be looking back to a model which owes more to Charles Dickens than to the world of the Super Information Highway. Clearly, as the continuing restructuring of the teaching profession takes place, the new teacher in the school of the future will require greater flexibility in teaching methodology, greater knowledge of the physiological, intellectual and cultural needs of pupils and a greater ability to utilize theory and practice in the consideration of relevant education. Overall there will be a requirement for a new professionalism which will not be developed adequately by the range of simplistic models currently being floated.

There is little doubt that the next few years will see a fight for the soul of teacher education. There is no doubt that many in the government have a clear and unambiguous view of where teacher education should go. However, experience argues that attack is often the best form of defence. If HEIs and schools are able to grasp the nettle and use examples of the best practice in mentoring, then the often pessimistic view of teacher educators over the past few years can be changed. As our research indicates, neither the schools nor the teachers want the system entirely to themselves. What is evident is that if the extremes of policy are challenged and the best of good practice promoted and advertised, then the future may be looked at in a more optimistic light. It is within the ideas developed in the following chapters that such optimism is grounded.

# References

Bolton, E (1994) 'Transitions in initial teacher training', in Wilkin, M and Sankey, D (eds) *Collaboration and Transition in Initial Teacher Training*, London: Kogan Page.

Centre for Contemporary Cultural Studies (1981) *Unpopular Education*, London: Hutchinson.

Cox, C B and Boyson, R (1970) *Black Paper*, London: Temple Smith.

Cox, C B and Dyson, A E (1977) *Black Papers Two*, London: Critical Quarterly Society.

DfE (1983) *Proposals for the Improvement of Teacher Quality*, London: DfE.

DfE (1984) *Accreditation of Teacher Education*, Circular 3/84, London: DfE.

DfE (1992) *Initial Teacher Training (Secondary Phase)*, Circular 9/92, London: DfE.

Glover, D, Gough, G, and Johnson, M (1994) *Towards a Taxonomy of Mentoring*, Mentoring and Tutoring Vol 2 No 2, Stoke on Trent: Trentham Books.

Kogan, M (1978) *The Politics of Educational Change*, Manchester: Manchester University Press.

McPherson, A and Raab, C D (1988) *Governing Education; A sociology of policy since 1945*, Edinburgh: Edinburgh University Press.

Mardle, G and Walker, M (1980) 'Strategies and structure: Some initial notes on teacher socialisation', in Woods, P (ed) *Teacher Strategies*, Beckenham: Croom Helm.

Moore, R (1994) 'Professionalism, expertise and control in teacher training', in Wilkin, M and Sankey, D *op cit*.

Wilkin, M (1990) 'The development of partnership in the United Kingdom', in Booth, M *et al.*, *Partnerships in Initial Teacher Training*, London: Cassell.

*Chapter 2*

# The Organizational Framework

*Derek Glover*

The concern in this investigation was to see how the newer patterns of school contribution to partnership were evolving to meet the requirement for at least 66 per cent of initial teacher training to be school-based. In all three higher education institutions which have ties with the case study schools, there had been a gradual development of links which have increased the time associates were spending in schools, but the responsibility for associate welfare and development had remained with the higher education tutors. There has been a need for fundamental organizational change to accommodate the new requirements, as the schools have undertaken a contractual obligation requiring the provision of opportunities for supervised professional and competence training (HMI, 1993). This responsibility has led to more formal organizational structures and a higher degree of accountability. At the same time, there is evidence of a change in attitudes as the philosophy of mentoring is more widely appreciated and the advantages of the integration of the work with whole school professional development are more widely appreciated.

The rationale for mentoring as a means of enhancing opportunities for the development of teaching skills and many of the practical issues in its development have been considered by, amongst others, Benton (1990), Hagger *et al.* (1994) and Wilkin and Sankey (1994). These studies have shown how students can be successfully supported by mentors who are committed to their role and who work within a favourable training environment.

## Involvement and Impetus

Staff in the collaborating schools have been involved in yet another aspect of coping with change as they have undertaken to train and assess more associates within the schools for a longer period each year. For the case study schools, the situation has been even more complex than that outlined by Pendry (1990) in her discussion of the development of the Oxford Internship Scheme, because of the pressures consequent upon recent legislative and administrative demands. Staff in the newer partnerships have also been faced with the adaptation of existing practices to meet the increased time and experiential training demands for initial teacher education as they became more responsible for the induction, competence development, professional growth, assessment and pastoral development of associate teachers. This additional work, outlined by Hagger *et al.* (1993), may have been imposed as a result of a senior management decision or may have come about because of a general agreement on the part of all staff. Willingness of staff to be involved, both within a department and in the school as an organization, appears to have been the most significant factor in securing a welcoming and beneficial experience for associate teachers, as discussed by Allsop (1994), who stresses the importance of the initial messages given by staff to associates. As examined in Chapter 1, research showed that in virtually all aspects of policy development and practice organization there is a spectrum of teaching environment which could help or inhibit this experience. The detail of this is given in Table 2.1, which summarizes mentors' perceptions of the support they have enjoyed from both school and department in the development of their role. They were asked to rank the support, with 1 as the highest level of support and 9 as the lowest. The concept of 'mentoring culture' was not defined.

**Table 2.1** *Mentors' perceptions of organizational support*

| Source of support | % ranked 1–3 | % ranked 6–9 |
| --- | --- | --- |
| School management | 51 | 15 |
| Department | 77 | 4 |
| School mentoring culture | 61 | 9 |
| Department mentoring culture | 71 | 8 |

Case study evidence supports the view that management, as observed by one mentor, frequently 'delegates downwards and then doesn't worry all the while there is no trouble'. The departmental support is likely to be higher than school support 'because we in the departments that volunteered are in a way pioneers and the others are gradually following', and the higher support from a school mentoring culture than from the management may indicate a 'grassroots feeling because we feel that colleagues may have become committed and we don't want to rock the boat'.

It would seem that where the school, department and individual mentor believe in the mutual benefits of a good practice, the associate teacher gains a great deal and this is most likely where the organizational culture is open and reliant upon staff acceptance of shared values based upon belief in the teacher training function, often as part of professional development.

Decision making in some case study schools was in the hands of a very small group of staff, while in others the staff as a whole agreed to be part of the new arrangement. In six of the case study schools, the first move towards acceptance of a contractual arrangement offered by the HEI was made by the head without prior staff consultation. Motivation for this included a perceived support for school improvement through staff involvement in training; a wish to be at the forefront of new developments which might bring a continuing, and possibly stronger, link with the HEI; and an attempt to enhance the reputation of the school with parents and governors in the belief that participation was a reflection of perceived quality. Three of these schools, and a further five who had become involved in other ways, had had a long association with the HEI concerned and saw the move towards a contractual relationship as a natural progression which could be achieved without major change. One head commented that, 'There was only limited concern at the way in which we would have to reorganize the teaching practice but when we actually began the work, we saw how things had changed'.

However, there is a clear difference between those schools where the change was made on the assumption that staff would agree to greater participation, and those where there was a longer period of negotiation. One school comments that, 'despite the previous involvement we were aware that strong unionization and awareness of the increased workload meant that we could only go along with the plan if the staff as a whole were willing'.

In six schools, the impetus for participation came from a member of the senior management team, usually the deputy who had previously undertaken the liaison with the HEI, but the approaches to staff were made in different ways. In one school the mentors believe that they 'were identified because the senior management team knew the qualities they were looking for'; in three the departments were told of the scheme on offer and asked to volunteer; and in four schools the case for participation was outlined to the staff as a whole by a member of the senior management team after negotiation with the HEI staff. One respondent felt that 'at no time was any great importance attached to the fact that the school would be paid for the involvement – it was sold on what it could do for the staff as a pilot, at the forefront of developments'.

In two schools, the prime movers were other than members of the senior management team. They appear to have developed their interest because of previous links with the HEI. In one school, the second in the English department had been involved with the HEI in developing course materials, and he approached the deputy involved in traditional teacher placement before the issue was discussed and agreed with the staff as a whole. The approach at another came directly from one of the college staff through two subject staff who then approached the senior management team 'in the belief that this would be to the greatest advantage of the school'.

Questionnaire responses show that 66 per cent of the respondents were consulted before the school accepted associate teachers. The introduction of the new scheme appears to have been with the agreement of unions in 11 of the schools, and with the approval of governors in seven. The responses from the former indicated that the involvement should be on a voluntary basis and there is evidence that union representatives in five schools rejected any payment to mentors at this stage, while those in three others were anxious to secure payment for the extra work undertaken. The governors believe that they have been involved where the 'change of policy was such that approval for the existing scheme could not be sufficient', and all approved participation, although two expressed reservations 'that it should not be detrimental to the progress of the pupils' and 'that it should be reviewed if the workload appeared to be too much for the staff'. In two schools, the views of parents were sought, and they did not dissent.

## Introducing Change

While the origin and impetus for participation in the contractual arrangements came mainly from the head or senior management, there are clear examples of evolution and revolution at work in the establishment of organizational practice. The continuum here is from the unplanned and piecemeal approach seen by one head at one extreme, where 'there was an assumption that the system would evolve as we attempted to meet the new demands of the HEI', to the planned whole school approach where a new scheme was started from scratch. This was exemplified in one school where the decision to take up to 11 associates was seen as part of a total revision of professional development policy reviewed by members of departments, individual teaching and ancillary staff and governors. This appears to have been a rare practice, because the potential of mentoring as part of whole staff development has become established in only two of the case study schools.

Evolution is a process of adaptation. Two professional mentors stated: 'the way in which we have worked with associates in the past has been changed as we have coped with new administrative and assessment methods', and 'we have well established patterns within departments and we have modified these to cope with what the HEI wants'. It does, however, bring with it new features – principally the need to determine the distribution of resources, especially where payment to mentors is concerned, but also the establishment of new staff relationships, where 'the mentors for their part see themselves very much as a team whose views are sought on the management of the scheme'. Schools have realized the need to develop these teams with the professional mentor to secure coherence and uniformity of approach within a complex scheme, but they have had to consider the structural implications.

Revolution appears to have occurred in those schools that have changed arrangements on a large scale. One school had had no teachers in training for four years, but agreed to take ten in the first term of the new arrangement. A professional mentor had been appointed to undertake the work, mentors selected after negotiation and a monitoring system put in place as part of the responsibility of the senior teacher for professional development. At another school, a similar number of associates were introduced after agreement with two HEIs for involvement in an arrangement that was acceptable to staff because of the offer of widespread accredited training, and a belief that major curriculum changes could be achieved with the additional classroom support provided during the training period. In each case, major policy documents were prepared, all stakeholders were consulted and the governors were involved.

In the schools that have previously had strong ties with the HEI there has been no pilot year. With one exception, the new associates have been integrated as the scheme has evolved and the questionnaire evidence suggests that they do not know of any change of emphasis or involvement. However, in five schools there has been some form of pilot as the details of the new scheme are worked through – for example, with only two associates in one department, and in another school, a list of departments awaiting training for mentoring has been established in the light of successful experience during a pilot period.

## Resource Allocation

While the contractual agreement between HEIs and the schools specifies the payment of a per capita fee for each associate trained, this is no guarantee that the resources will be transferred in such a way that the mentor is paid for the additional work undertaken. Of the 20 case study schools, only seven return a significant proportion of the fee to the mentoring staff; eight have a system of varying complexity which returns some payment or time in lieu to mentoring departments; and the remaining five use the resources for departmental or whole school benefit but with no personal payment for mentoring duties. Table 2.2 summarizes the variety of resource transfer arrangements made for the 100 mentors who responded to the questionnaire.

**Table 2.2** *Resource transfer to mentors*

| Resource Transfer | % Respondents |
| --- | --- |
| Mentors are paid for the work | 48 |
| Mentors are paid for each associate | 28 |
| Mentors are given time for the work | 21 |
| Mentors are guaranteed non-contact time | 30 |
| Mentors are paid and given time | 8 |

Where the resources are paid to the mentors, in three of the 20 case study schools with appropriate job descriptions and agreements, the payment ranges from £320 to £1,000 per mentor. The higher payment is made where each mentor is responsible for two associates. The lowest direct payment is part of a package which splits the resources between mentor, supporting department and the professional mentor. Indeed, there is a complex arrangement within all the schools which attempts to give something to school, department and all personnel involved in teacher training. In one school which has been evolving a scheme which meets the needs of professional development, the payment is converted to time and each mentor is allocated two periods per week, but she also receives some 'college training credit' for personal professional development. As in three of the 'direct payment' schools, the residue of the fee income is paid to the professional mentor either to support time, an honorarium, or the support of professional development activities.

Where payments are made indirectly, the schools have a formula which attempts to balance the varying additional time and resource demands consequent upon a revised mentoring procedure. These arrangements are illustrated in one school where the fees support a time allocation to the deputy head (as professional mentor), £123 per subject department involved for additional books and materials needed, and £500 to each head of department to deploy as the department agrees for mentor supervision. In another, the deputy head explained that funds are allocated to 'provide for an enhanced salary for the professional mentor so as to reflect the responsibility and status of the post, to allow mentors to attend training and to engage in INSET to perform their roles as mentors, to provide refreshments for associates at particular times of the year, eg, parents' evenings, to build up a library for staff development, and to benefit the whole school'. In one school with a long association with the HEI, an attempt has been made to cost the activity with the notional timing of hours of contact per term used as part of the formula which gives 15 per cent of the income to a central fund 'which becomes part of the undetermined pot for school benefit', pays for the additional involvement of the professional mentor in assessment and administration, and then allocates an hourly payment for five hours in the first term, 11 hours in the main block practice, and five hours in the summer term. The professional mentor suggests that this reflects a wish 'on the part of the staff as a whole to be able to have an associate for part of the year or to organize more flexible allocation of time and interest within departments'. Although payments of this sort have been made in one school, the professional mentor believes that they are seen by many colleagues to be 'totally inadequate for the amount of time which we have given and in many ways it isn't worth the finance officer's efforts, but it seems to placate people when they are asked to be involved'.

In those schools which do not make any personal payment to mentors, this appears to be rationalized by senior management on a basis that 'it is morally wrong for a person to be paid for mentoring when they are only extending their normal duties as a teacher', or 'the system is so complex and we feel that we need to recognize the contribution that all the staff make to the work of mentoring – it can vary from term to term and associate to associate'. A more positive view is expressed by one head, where 'mentoring relies on goodwill; if you start paying for it, it changes the emphasis totally and could be a cause of tension'. In all except one of the case study schools where there has been some comment on the decision not to make payments to mentors, this view is attributed to the head, for example as 'the head is opposed to the idea of payment and no payment is ever likely to be made to mentors', but there is evidence of a contrary shift of staff opinion and some departments have agreed to pay mentors in recognition of their additional duties. Where the decision not to pay was taken more openly, a staff member commented that this was because 'we as a staff felt that there was so much whole school involvement in the training and we wanted the money to be used to help us all'; the funding is split four ways between professional mentor time, INSET opportunities for mentoring staff, improvements to benefit the associates (this year by refurbishing a work base), and departmental resources. There is evidence that two of the case study schools making no direct payments have kept the debate from the staff by 'offering some compensation for time worked beyond that which is contractual', and 'by assuming that there has been no change in arrangements because the staff believe that we are working with a pilot scheme and senior management have not told them otherwise'.

Evidence of recent change suggests that schools which have not previously made direct payments to mentors are beginning to do so. One deputy head suggested that this was 'in response to the increase in moneys into school from the partnership and in recognition of the increase in work associated with mentoring'. While this is the only school which appears to have recognized an increase in funding, it is one of four which have been able to devise a scheme of payment which meets the demands for flexibility of mentoring contact, possibly by different staff, through the school year, and it reflects the move towards some recompense for the additional work 'which is not what we would always have done but the extra which arises from developing a new scheme within the schools'.

## Time Management

As indicated in Table 2.2, some additional time allocation is used as an alternative to direct payment in a minority of schools. The information on the case study schools indicates that eight of the professional mentors have an allocation of time, six in lieu of the fact that they are not paid a supplement for their work, and two because this is regarded as an additional responsibility. There is a specific weekly time allocation in four schools. This varies from two periods per associate mentored, described as 'sufficient for the extra paperwork', to one lesson of guaranteed protected time free from cover duties which is 'valued by the mentors but is seen as only a small part of the overall time given to associates'.

The other 16 schools make a variety of arrangements which show the differing philosophies behind senior management views of mentoring. The more extreme views may be seen in accounts of eight schools where, for example, 'the mentors are getting paid in lieu of time' , 'the load is to be carried along with the function', and 'no time is allocated because this is work to be undertaken out of school except for the professional mentor who has an additional administrative burden'. In the other eight schools there is a more sensitive recognition that the time allocation may 'not be practicable because of the varying demands across the year and the late notification of the associates and their programme', and 'the need for the coincidence of free time'. Even here there is evidence of compromise arrangements, for example where the senior management felt that 'although there was pressure on mentors to give time over and above what is necessary in the early part of the year, there would be gains for them at the end of the year with associates taking on more of the lessons of mentors...and arrangements would be made for cover at particular times when mentors needed it'.

## Management Structures

The introduction of a major responsibility has had management implications in all schools, although three of the 20 schools convey in some
form the impression of one head that mentoring is 'a bolt-on to normal
organization – they look at it as just another bit of administration'. In
two schools the management is concentrated in the hands of senior staff
where the 'head makes the key decisions because he carries the final
contractual responsibility and because he works with a deputy as professional mentor', and where 'the system is controlled by the deputy head
as professional mentor with a clear link to the head who sees the system
as a reaction to immediate needs rather than as part of permanent
policy'. In both schools the degree of other senior staff involvement
appears to be limited.

In ten schools the professional mentor is a member of the senior
management team and as such is able to influence policy without organizational change. This may convey an impression of central administration and policy determination for example, where a mentor felt that
'there is a clear feeling that the whole scheme is centrally controlled and
mentor input is peripheral to the making of policy'. The 'ease of decision making and the flexibility which has been fundamental to the
development of a scheme which looks after 11 associates each year' is
however recognized in another school by a mentor in her assessment of
management.

In all the remaining schools the professional mentor follows a delegated role which is more or less concerned with administrative tasks
according to the philosophy, time available and previous practice of the
staff concerned. At one school with organization on an ad hoc team
basis, this is a senior teacher who is involved with a middle management
planning group; at another the professional mentor role is taken by a
head of department who then reports by invitation to the senior
management team; and at a third the professional mentor was a main
professional grade teacher who was then promoted to be in charge of
initial teacher education in recognition of its policy significance.
Relationships and consultative processes vary from school to school, but
those schools which have a downward delegated professional mentor
appear to have more strongly developed mentoring teams. The internal
management of the scheme is the domain of the professional mentor,
and the management style adopted by the professional mentor has a

significant impact on the status and the interpretation of the role of the mentor. One respondent expressed the view that if 'the mentoring process is tied in with other aspects of staff development' and mentors are considered to have a 'positive contribution to the management of the scheme', then the organization is collaborative. However, if the mentors are treated as separate entities and the professional mentor merely passes on information, the scheme tends to be poorly integrated into school management systems. In the five schools where the professional mentor role is undertaken by a deputy head, there is a tendency for the management of the associates to be more firmly placed in the hands of the mentors and this can lead to a lack of coherence in practice where, as seen by one mentor, 'the professional mentor, a deputy head, coordinates the process but once the mentors are in place the departments do most of the organizing'.

The integration of initial teacher education and the school development planning process provides some indication of the structural changes within school management. In eight of the case study schools, the initial teacher education work is recognized as part of the school development plan – a sign that the commitment is recognized as being relatively long-term and with staffing and resource implications. It is significant that three of the four schools associated with HEIs which offer some accreditation for mentoring, are included within the group which have an emphasis on development planning.

In only five schools has the work become integrated with other aspects of professional development policy including INSET and appraisal, but where this has been introduced 'staff have become aware of the benefits of the flexibility and the increase in training opportunities for all staff, not just the mentors'. Where there is a relationship between appraisal and initial teacher training it is through the establishment of targets, including mentoring experience. This is the basis of the view of one professional mentor that she 'would seek to persuade heads of department to change mentoring plans if a member of staff would gain career benefit as a result'. Two of the schools use the associates as part of the annual evaluation process and one makes time available for mentors and associates to evaluate the mentoring scheme to include its impact upon the school. Two schools also integrate mentoring opportunities as part of their evaluation and quality assurance provision in the belief that 'the associates are an element in our experience for the pupils and we need to be sure that we are meeting their needs in a way which allows them to give the most they can to the pupils'. Our evidence suggests that this may be a second stage of development requiring more time and confidence in the operation of the scheme. One deputy head, a professional mentor, cautioned that the senior staff of schools do not wish to 'convey the view that we are irretrievably committed to something about which we have serious doubts with the present funding'.

## The Nature of Involvement

Most of the schools investigated sought a voluntary element in the appointment of mentors. From the case study interviews it would seem that 58 mentors out of a possible 85 (68 per cent) felt that they had volunteered for the role. Responses to the questionnaire showed a higher percentage, 91 per cent, of volunteers, but the nature of volunteering is not defined. Positive involvement requires the mentors to act in relation to an invitation or advertisement which has occurred where in one school the professional mentor comments that 'true volunteers are sought on a year-to-year basis – when we know the subject areas we require then we go through the process of interview and appointment'. Our evidence suggests that this has happened in only three of the schools.

Negotiation about involvement and the allocation of duties within the department is mentioned as normal procedure in 12 of the schools, and is believed to have minimized tension. Direct approaches from the professional mentor which have occurred in five schools may actually exacerbate problems where, for example, one head of department commented that 'the professional mentor approaches individual staff and asks for their cooperation before talking matters over with the head of department – this led to an unsatisfactory experience for associates within the maths department'. In three of these schools, however, the approach was from the professional mentor to 'those who had a genuine skill and desire to do the work' and for whom 'there had been negotiation at senior staff level so that the departments were aware of what was going on'.

Job descriptions are used in connection with the role in five schools and are part of the appraisal process in two of these. Mentors variously comment that 'the work might be of use for the cv', 'it provides an opportunity to focus reflection on our work', 'it might help when it comes to looking for another job', and 'it gives a strong interest to diversify the teaching pattern'. While this would suggest that they do not rank the work highly in securing promotion, staff of the three schools linked to an accreditation scheme with their local HEI are on a waiting list for involvement in mentoring. Only three of the heads would look at former mentoring experience in seeking new appointments, and only one would advertise for staff with this experience.

The professional mentors appear to have been recruited by either 'designation' by the head (seven schools), usually by the addition of the role to that of other work undertaken by deputy heads; 'appointed', usually by internal advertisement or approach to a senior teacher or head of faculty (nine schools); or 'inherited' in so far as they had previously been the link for placements by the HEI. Of this latter group of four deputies or senior teachers, only one appears to be involved in other aspects of professional or curriculum development – evidence of the bolt-on nature of much initial training work.

The organization of the scheme does lead to tensions between staff. For example, 'one mentor was told by a senior manager at the school that the head of department was not necessarily the most appropriate person for the job as the head of department had already got a lot of administration and other responsibilities'. In another school, 'although the mentor has only been teaching for three years, the professional mentor felt that she was an appropriate appointment even if it meant that more experienced staff did not have the chance to undertake the work'. Associates are aware of the pressures which mentoring brings and felt that heads of department were not always able to give the time required. They were similarly critical of deputy heads as professional mentors 'because they have other duties and see us as administrative work rather than as real people'.

## Impact

One head felt that the impact of the enlarged mentoring activity and the revised initial teacher education scheme 'put a heavy pressure on the schools which, in the interest of the pupils, they may have to consider as an unwanted burden'. The management of reputation and the avoidance of unwanted parental criticism has affected the way in which the associates link into the school. One mentor cautioned that the 'training is now done within the school and the mentors are the people who have to live with the results, they can't hand things over to the college in the way that they used to do'. Staff within schools are thus aware of the pressures for the associates to contribute to, rather than detract from, the learning process. Indeed, the professional mentor in the one college of further education in the sample felt that it has 'become increasingly difficult to secure a placement for students because the department, the students and the mentor are worried that results might fall as a result'.

It would seem that there is a continuum of experience from the uncoordinated to the totally planned, and practice in the schools investigated, although tending to the latter, has provided evidence of some of the disruption which results. Staff admit that 'there is less risk than previously because we are the ones who are responsible for what occurs, although it is now more difficult if we have got a weak associate who needs more care than we are able to give without detriment to our real work'. They still speak of the 'time lost in the early days of a practice when we have to do so much to support the associate', 'impact of a large associate presence on a small school where the parents might complain at the way in which the normal teaching programme is disrupted', and 'coping with the problems which stem from those colleagues who are not involved but who are quick to point out problems which may arise from time to time'.

Where the picture is much more positive, in 12 of the schools, the benefits listed include 'the availability of additional staff in the classroom and in the school as a whole – it increases pupil support', 'the new ideas which are something for the regular staff to consider when they have time to reflect', 'the possibility of additional input for assessment, team teaching, project and individual work', 'the opportunity for departmental development with additional help', 'the avoidance of the disruptive impact of turning the students loose with a group', and 'the change from the student to the associate culture'. Schools also mention the involvement of associates in extra-mural activities, music, drama and personal and social education over a much longer period.

The schools which have planned their course in conjunction with the information from the HEIs appear to have developed a gentle induction into teaching, explained by one associate through 'pairs, and then individual work with small groups, and then leaving us alone with the full class from time to time in such a way that we did not feel exposed and the class did not see us as something different'. The case studies show that seven schools maintain an audit of associate exposure to classes and individuals. The degree of sophistication of this varies from a simple list of classes taught by an associate in any one year, through a departmental list of pupils taught, to the most comprehensive list of pupils taught by associates over the time they have been in the school. One school reports two adverse parental comments in a year, another three from parents and two from pupils, but by and large the deputy head felt that 'the associates do bring gains in enthusiasm, team teaching and in class support and the pupils benefit more than lose!' There are concerns however, at the impact of ten associates in one school, 11 in another and eight in another where one non-mentoring member of staff felt 'the staff could become swamped, the situation unreal and the associates gain a false view of coping on their own'.

The responses to the associate questionnaires are an indication of the impact of the training upon those who are now going through the revised process. Associates now assess the HEI input in the development of skills and the provision of experiences generally lower than that of schools. Although this is to be expected on the grounds of contact time alone, some associates fail to see a progression from HEI to school, and some school staff are critical of a system which appears to them to cover a more limited range of subject knowledge and pedagogic skills. This situation is made more difficult where the professional mentors, usually because of the pressure on their time, have been unable to arrange a professional studies programme within the school. However, associates generally recognize that this progression is taking place and show that they understand the role of the HEI and school as joint providers. Table 2.3 summarizes the views of the 1994 cohort of PGCE students. This is based upon responses from 180 associates.

**Table 2.3** *Associate perceptions of PGCE course*

| Feature | % positive responses |
| --- | --- |
| Importance of HEI contribution | 78.5 |
| Tutors and mentors have common criteria | 62.5 |
| HEI and school complement each other | 57.7 |
| Course has lived up to expectations | 80.2 |
| Strong commitment before course began | 62.0 |
| Strong commitment after PGCE course | 58.3 |

The contribution of mentoring to these perceptions can be judged from some of the open comment made by associates at the end of the evaluation. At one extreme one associate reported, 'I was disappointed with the lack of mentor support. I was basically left entirely to my own devices and had to muddle through. Initially this was worrying but I learned through trial and error. Basically my mentor did not have time to take on an associate as he was preoccupied with other duties. I was expecting a more supportive and involved approach'.

The opposite viewpoint from another associate confirms the value of a changed organization in a school where the positive culture has encouraged participation: 'The support of the mentor was at the heart of the progress I made but I did gain a great deal from the others in the department and the staff room in general. I felt that it was a school that knew why it had got us there but it didn't belittle us and we had status and an input from the start'.

## Interaction

Overall there is evidence that associate experience may be affected by two organizational features. Where the introduction of the mentoring scheme has been agreed by the staff after consideration of all the issues and as part of the shared value system of the school, a positive philosophy prevails. This is shown at Portland school where 'much of the time has been spent in trying to establish shared values – they have always been there but now we are aware of the togetherness we can offer', and where a member of staff who was not a specified mentor commented 'the pupils gain from fresh faces, new ideas and additional pairs of hands with a tremendous contribution during the busy Spring term'.

Additionally, where the ITE work has been considered to be part of an integrated professional development programme for the staff, and particularly where this programme is organized by the person who is also the professional mentor, there is a positive view of the benefits of involvement. Again at Portland, 'the staff development planning is based upon appraisal and recognition of an initial teacher training target is given second priority next to subject-based work...there are three applicants for every one place because the programme offers so much, like counselling, reflection and so on...'.

These aspects contribute to the experiences discussed in Chapter 8 –

only schools which have a discussed and agreed policy for mentors as part of a positive staff development policy appear to offer supportive environments on mentor, department and whole school levels. The elements of shared values and integrated professional development may not co-exist, and four possible situations are suggested in Table 2.4 which relates these elements to the nature of associate experience in the case study schools.

**Table 2.4** *Organizational elements and associate experience*

| Mentoring as part of shared values of staff | Integration of professional development programme | Associate experience of whole school attitudes |
| --- | --- | --- |
| Discussed and agreed | Integrated management | Positive, planned, integrated |
| Discussed and agreed | Disparate management | Positive but liaison needed |
| Imposed | Integrated management | Subjective but planned |
| Imposed | Disparate management | Subjective, fragmented |

While the organizational framework may inhibit a positive experience in some schools, the associate may be protected from this by the attitude, competence and status of the mentor.

The case study reports in the next chapter provide evidence of the way in which the organizational framework of the schools has developed to handle the new requirements, and shows much of the debate within schools as these pressures impact upon daily life for staff and associates. They demonstrate how common perceptions promote supportive structures for associates.

# References

Allsop, T (1994) 'The language of partnership', in Wilkin, M and Sankey, D (eds) *Collaboration and Transition in Initial Teacher Training*, London: Kogan Page.

Benton P (ed.) (1990) *The Oxford Internship Scheme*, London: Calouste Gulbenkian Foundation.

Hagger, H, Burn, K and McIntyre, D (1993) *The School Mentor Handbook*, London: Kogan Page.

Hagger, H, McIntyre, D and Burn, K (1994) *The Management of Student Teachers' Learning*, London: Kogan Page.

HMI (1993) *The Secondary PGCE in Universities*, London: HMSO.

Pendry, A (1990) 'The process of change' in Benton, P (ed.) *The Oxford Internship Scheme*, London: Calouste Gulbenkian Foundation.

Wilkin, M and Sankey, D (1994) *Collaboration and Transition in Initial Teacher Training*, London: Kogan Page.

*Chapter 3*

# Case Studies

*Derek Glover*

These case studies have been selected from the 20 schools investigated because they illustrate the way in which mentoring is being managed within differing philosophical and organizational paramaters. They are offered to give a picture of the complexity of interaction within schools, and to provide evidence of the differing environments within which teacher education is taking place. They are not intended as exemplars of good or bad practice but rather reflect the reality of advantages and disadvantages for the associate arising from the diversity of mentoring cultures. All the case studies have been abridged to meet editorial needs. The titles given are fictitious to respect the wishes of those schools which so readily and openly agreed to offer their organization for investigation.

## Case Study A: Low Moor School

### Discussed and agreed by staff. Integrated management

*The outline detail of arrangements at Low Moor school shows how a common philosophy of training responsibilities and the integration of staff development provide a totally supportive environment for the associates involved.*

The school has worked with two colleges for the past 11 years and the head said that 'it was a natural progression for us to move from placement to fully mentoring institutions – the staff knew of our involvement and the college knew the standards we would give and expect'. There was some involvement in the setting up of arrangements with one of the colleges because the deputy head (DH), who acts as professional mentor, had been a member of the college liaison committee and was prepared to work on the pilot scheme and with the committee of organization which had set up the scheme. The view of the deputy head was that 'being in at the policy end has been a help, but we also know that we might gain from the opportunity to mould the way things develop – we were also keen to use mentoring as a major force for curriculum change within the school'. The responsibility of the DH for all aspects of staff development including appraisal, INSET, staff development planning and initial teacher training, gives an integrated approach which means that all aspects of development are an opportunity for some staff enhancement. A subject mentor commented that 'the school has always believed in providing opportunities for the staff to get further training and they have worked hard to provide a means of accreditation at one of the colleges'.

The school took the decision for full involvement after discussion with the union groups, the heads of department and then the staff as a whole. A staff mentor said, 'It was believed that we might gain and the terms were very favourable – recognition meant that we felt valued by the senior staff'. Subject mentors were appointed after a call for volunteers following a presentation to the staff, and there are two mentors in each curriculum area at present with a reserve of staff awaiting the opportunity if possible. The professional mentor reflected the positive view of mentoring: 'It may seem that with 11 associates we have a lot of students, but we don't see them as such – they are additional members of the staff who help with the development of the pupils' learning – the pupils are used to them to the extent that they are just additional members of the team'. All staff who have embarked on the scheme have enjoyed the work, largely because of their commitment from the start and also because of the way in which they are part of an ongoing scheme with a programme of meetings with associates, other mentors and the professional mentor. On balance, 'these meetings are a nuisance but then they are an opportunity to meet with the others and to think about those things which are a bit beyond the day-to-day business of the classroom and the pressures don't seem the same'. Mentors are paid for the role and all money paid to the school by the colleges is ploughed back into the scheme as payments to mentors, supply cover for certain meetings, the enhancement of the staff professional development library and to pay for the work of associates with other members of staff, eg, for work with equal opportunities as a curriculum concern. The mentors also have two periods of non-contact time per associate. The current rate of £450 per mentor plus £150 per year for each associate mentored is seen as generous by subject mentors 'and can only come about because we have so many associates and because the top-slicing for school administration is minimal – indeed, I reckon that the costs of the professional mentor are met more from staff development than from participation in this scheme'.

The scheme presented few problems because it was introduced by the senior management team as being worthy of serious consideration, giving opportunities, time and recognition for the work. The head believed that the philosophy of creating 'professional training opportunities so that something could be offered as appraisal targets were developed was an important motivator for us'. The scheme was readily approved by the governors, has been well received by HMI and has met no opposition from the parents. One subject mentor reported that 'there have been one or two comments from pupils who have had a break in continuity with staff they very much respect, but then there have been as many counter comments when the associates finish their spell with us'. The impact on the school is generally positive. The scheme is seen by the mentors to be an opportunity to think about the work underway and the way in which it is taught, in a situation where there may often be two people in the classroom supporting the pupils. The use of the phrases 'two pairs of hands', and 'my student' indicate that there is a close relationship in the planning, delivery and monitoring of associate work. The cost in time is considerable, particularly where a weaker associate may not be having regular support from the college and remedial work has to be maintained by the mentor and professional mentor. 'It is a good scheme when all parties are pulling together, but I have had one weak student this year – he has taken hours of my time and the response from the college has been minimal – at the end of the day the responsibility is to the pupils rather than the students and I can see a time when we might need to say to the professional mentor that enough was enough'. The outcomes of the new scheme are beneficial in that associates enjoy a greater and continuing support, are seen teaching on a more frequent basis and are helped with competence problems more regularly than was possible with the previous pattern of college support. At the same time, associates comment that they now have a very limited 'fallback to support us at college – the college staff are not as involved as previously and the mentor relationship is very close, at times a little stifling'. Another comment from an associate was that 'the system is ok if you have a good mentor and things are going well, but there can be difficulties if you are tied by ideas which contrast with your own – I haven't rocked the boat whilst I have been here because it is not the culture of the place to do so, but I have felt frustrated by a fundamental difference of philosophy over the nature of my subject, RE'.

For the associates, there is evidence that integrated serial and block practice presents an opportunity for both individual and group progression, with associates gaining from peer support and the sharing of ideas between themselves, and between the mentors as groups. One advantage has been that classroom management has been less of a problem in training because they are developing alongside the mentor with the groups for whom they will be responsible. Mentors have maintained their contact with their teaching groups, and staff, associates and pupils have gained from the exchange of ideas which has been prompted by the development of opportunities for differentiation in learning style and student experience. One mentor spoke of 'a more intense enjoyment of the teaching situation at associate and pupil level'. The associates have appreciated the mutual support gained where there is more than one associate in a department and the 'generally positive views that mentors have had of our work'.

The staff development aspect is important and, as the scheme has not met with staff resistance, there is a readiness on the part of staff to undertake the work and the opportunities for reflective practice have been developed to the full. There is a feeling that the first year of the work has been dominated by the issues of mechanics and the organization of time. All involved speak of the time required if the mentoring process is to be of mutual benefit. Much of the time has been spent in the planning process, eg, in developing agreement on the assessment of competences and the way in which associate interviews, further training and the match between the school and college professional development programmes can be achieved.

Links to the school professional development programme are made through the appraisal process which identifies targets through consideration of job descriptions against actual experience, and through the expression of individual needs. The mentoring experience is a means of meeting some of these specified training needs and through 'Investors in People' the school shows that it is using opportunities as they present themselves. The continuation of mentoring with a stronger link to the colleges is seen as a part of the professional development scheme. The training provided by the colleges has been variable in quality according to subject, and there is some wish for a coherent policy across all departments – this was seen as a particular problem during the Autumn term, when initial training programmes at college and school needed synchronization at a time when school demands differed from the college timetable. The initial training for mentors was 'well organized, of good quality and appropriate to our needs in a new situation', and there is a view that 'following the intensive action needed during a very brief period of preparation, we may now go into a more reflective phase and look at the way in which we are approaching the work on a more philosophical level'.

The experience appears to have been positive for the school, which has a heavy commitment to its training role. The associates have been happily integrated with the staff as a whole and the outcomes are seen as 'rewarding staff development work', 'increasing mentoring skills which help when you are working with the pupils and which lead to different learning techniques', 'the development of new ideas of both content and presentation', 'the encouragement of self-learning', and the availability 'of more practical help when you are working alongside the students and pupils'. The cost in time for all aspects of planning and preparation and the constant mentoring is 'high but with competent associates there is some payback as the year goes on and if we are able to use the third term properly, we may feel real benefit', but the overall gain is in the provision of opportunities for enhanced staff development, especially if real partnership develops with the colleges. The pupils appear to have gained from the wider experience they are given and the associates take a full share in meetings with parents to underline their professionality and competence. As a result, parental comment has been 'favourable especially where we have had a higher level of help and supervision and we are building on the new relationships'.

## Case Study B: The Wake School

### Discussed and agreed by staff. Disparate management

*Although the associates have a consistent and coherent experience because of the common support from all staff, there is a hint of missed opportunities whereby integrated staff development and ITE might be beneficial to staff and associates.*

This is a 11–16 five form entry school on a split site and serving a large council estate. Formerly the allocation of students to subject areas was a matter for negotiation between HEI subject staff and the departments within the school with the deputy head as the 'link person'. The head then negotiated with the heads of department to set up a structure that enabled the department to have students but recognized that the work, as expressed by one mentor, needed to be 'undertaken by people with a commitment and time for the task'.

The decision to take students had been agreed by the senior management team following the presentation of the scheme by the deputy head, who had been associated with the HEI curriculum group for a long period and who had been one of the advisory committee setting up the new structure. He agreed that 'it might not have been acceptable, after all, we are a strongly unionized staff and there was some feeling that we were being asked to do the work that the HEI should be doing. There was also a view that we ought not give the pupils any more instability than they had already – the decision to pair mentor and student without using other staff arose from this'. The senior management team gave the changed scheme a high profile and the professional mentor 'sold involvement on the basis of what it was doing for the school – new faces and ideas, additional help during the spring term in particular, and the opportunity for us to get something from the HEI link'.

There is no time allocation for the staff involved in mentoring. A mentor explained that the 'job is seen as out of school and a matter for us to arrange within the greater flexibility that having a student brings'. The deputy head, who also acts as professional mentor, has ten per cent of his time paid for by the income so that 'there is some recognition of the extra work that has to be done within the school day – you can't observe a lesson if the class isn't there'. The mentors are paid according to the contract hours negotiated with the HEI, currently five hours during the term. In effect, as one mentor comments, 'I worked many more hours than the contract defines – in the first few days of the block practice I was doing nothing without my shadow, but as the term has gone on he has developed an independence that allows me some time for standing back and reflecting on what it is all about'.

Staff have differing perceptions of the payment as shown by the unwilling-ness of some to volunteer 'because it is only playing into the hands of the government in further pressurizing the staff of schools'. Each department has had a small supplement for resources such as photocopying and additional texts if they have had a student during the year.

The management of the scheme is in the hands of the deputy head who, as professional tutor, 'maintains a link with the HEI link tutor, and with subject tutors if necessary, and with the staff of the school so that we offer a coherent programme for students. This does include a weekly session with each student for review and planning and a joint session on professional development matters'. The students are treated as full members of staff and take a part in duties, and appear on published rotas. Policy matters are dealt with by the professional mentor and the head, and 'governors have been informed, but on the basis that we are gaining prestige from the involvement'.

The school has not yet integrated the professional development role, main-tained by the other deputy, with the training role, but the mentors are beginning to argue that this ought to be a possibility. One subject mentor comments, 'I have gained enormously from having a student – it has made me think about the rationale for action, the way we approach learning and the way in which we handle ideas – I have no doubt that I am a better teacher (even if a very tired one) as a result of this term'. The new involvement does not appear on the school development plan but the deputy head acknowledges 'that it is a favourable thing to have as part of appraisal'.

The staff are true volunteers on a year-to-year basis. Three, all from one department, were 'a source of concern to the head of department until we showed him that having three students doubled our strength when we were coping with all the assessment processes, and that the department would gain from the team activities we had thought about together'. Other staff have asked to go on a waiting list for involvement, and there has been pressure on the deputy head to open negotiations with other HEIs for subjects not currently on offer. To date no staff have been recruited with mentoring in mind, but the deputy head was 'aware of the change it has brought to people and would certainly look at involvement when interviewing new staff'.

Although there has been some negative staff comment about the degree of disruption, there is no evidence that this has occurred. The way in which the mentors have developed the association of themselves with students and taught groups has given a partnership approach evidenced in the 'literature workshops, the pre-GCSE interviews, the double marking of all assignments in years 10 and 11 and the joint teaching from time to time'. Whilst there has been no attempt to monitor the impact on pupils one subject mentor feels that this is would be impossible and suggests an unrealistic anxiety because of the flexibility of setting arrangements, and the fact that nobody has said 'I reckon that the pupils have gained'. Another mentor comments that 'we have shown the parents that the students are real contributors by using them at parents' evenings as supporters in what we have to say'.

The four mentors are all volunteers and have a high degree of motivation. One has no other responsibilities – 'the lowest of the low within the department, but I felt that it was time that I gave something back'. One is a year head, but I have determined to involve myself in something other than the pastoral dimension', and the other two are 'middle ranking, long serving and in need of some new challenge'. The role has 'grown by understanding rather than by definition, but the mentors here had three training sessions at the HEI and meet each term with the deputy head for administrative and methodological discussion'. The three members of one department have 'an informal working arrangement which helps in matters like assessment and schemes of work', but the single member of the maths department has found that the 'job is a compromise between what I and the HEI want and what the head of department thinks we should be giving'. These informal discussions have led to a greater understanding of the skills involved. 'At the moment we are very much amateurs in doing the job properly – we know what we ought to be doing but counselling, finding the right balance between praise and pushing, and helping students to understand the learning process, which we only understand partially, is not easy'. The mentors are aware that the termly meetings sponsored by the HEI help with skills development and they 'see them as both reassuring and as helping to set new targets – although there are more needs than these alone'. However, one mentor said 'I really feel that I need to be assessed in what I am doing because I am so much of a beginner in all this – our own competences are in need of review'. Indeed, this is the only school where the staff had recognized that their work might be capable of competence mapping.

Their motivation is summed up in one comment. 'I have worked in the school for 11 years and I realize that I am becoming rather set – the students give an opportunity to bring in some fresh blood, even if only temporarily, and they have enabled us to rethink our ideas in a way that has made the department more lively – I suppose that it is professional development on the hoof'. Another mentor has suggested that 'the mentoring role gives you a feeling of worth, a bit of self-esteem in that somebody is recognizing the contribution you can make to the development of another adult'. All four mentors have family commitments locally and all agree that they took on the role in an attempt to add diversity to their experience without any motivation for promotion or additional payment. 'The money is derisory when the time taken is added up, but I have got something out of sharing the work with interested adults – their interest is its own reward, and I have enjoyed being the mother protector again.'

The system appears to be operating in a very flexible way within the school. The mentors speak of 'autonomy in doing what I want to do within the limits set by the subject requirements of CATE as interpreted by the HEI tutor'. Relationships with the HEI are seen as 'distant under the new dispensation', but the mentors do use agreed HEI procedures for assessment, review and report writing. Accountability within the school is not seen as a problem by mentors 'because the students are working within a framework as co-teachers and we don't want to go beyond our limits', but 'we are not sure where we stand with regard to the HEI – what would they do if we didn't deliver the goods, or if we went along a path which might be anti-CATE?' There has been no evidence of failure of staff to cooperate in cross-curricular activities during the current term and two of the mentors have been approached by heads of department wishing to have student help. The system is clearly understood, and because of the open way in which staff now discuss what has happened, the deputy believes that there is 'hope that it will develop, become integrated with our other professional development work and give us the opportunity to provide a bit of additional challenge for some staff – there is no shortage of volunteers'.

Above all, 'there is now a belief that we have gained from the experience and that there will be some further gains as we look at the professional development implications for the staff involved.' But, as one mentor comments, the 'costs in time have been enormous – for one week at the start of term I felt that I was not my own keeper and that the student was a permanent appendage and drain on my mental and emotional energy' and the 'responsibility is one you don't appreciate until you take it on'.

The staff as a whole are aware of the changes that have occurred and are beginning to consider a collective response. They recognize that there have been gains and they want the opportunity to take part in the scheme and develop further the benefits it has brought, but they are anxious that all the money paid by the HEI should be returned to the staff concerned and that the scheme should not 'allow the senior management to make more out of us on the side when we are having enough problems anyway'. They are also anxious that the arrangement should continue on a paired basis rather than that there should be any return to responsibility undertaken by the department as a whole. The senior management have seen the advantages of enhanced expectation and standing on the part of participants and are hopeful that the scheme will develop further. But they are also aware that the time commitment has been considerable and that the payback in time release later in the course is no longer a possibility, because the staff feel that they continue to be the trainers and that they need to support students more fully than in the past throughout their course. There is some move towards incorporating professional development targets with the mentoring opportunities, but this may be hampered if the HEI is not able to determine the placements it will need well ahead of time. At the same time, the partnership with the HEI is growing. The long-term view is that there might be a more substantial payback through professional development, INSET or other staff training possibilities.

## Case Study C: Churchover School

### Imposed participation. Integrated management

*Arrangements at this school reflect the strong leadership of the head who, although asking the staff about involvement, had a clear view of the benefits of ITE participation. To ensure coherence, this work was then linked, initially under her supervision, to staff development planning, but there are some signs that staff feel that they have been pushed into a new scheme. Some associates feel that they may not be wanted by their departments although there is no evidence that this has affected relationships or the success of the experience.*

This five form entry comprehensive school in a mixed housing area on the outskirts of a large city was originally a grammar school and is still seen by the local people as maintaining 'good grammar traditions'. The link with colleges of higher education has been developed over the past 20 years but is contextualized by one mentor who said that contact should be 'maintained in such a way that the work with the students should not get in the way of the school as a whole'. Formerly the negotiation of placement was undertaken by the departmental staff of the relatively local colleges and the network of known people in departments at the school. The introduction of a contract system has provided an opportunity for the head to change the emphasis from 'teacher training to teacher education as part of the approach to staff development'.

The head was anxious to involve as many staff as possible in the activity, and planned a presentation to the full staff in collaboration with the senior management team and the professional development coordinator. She said: 'The view was that we wanted to develop a better approach to meeting targets identified in appraisal and that we needed to have the best possible links with those colleges which could provide INSET opportunities. It was suggested that payments might be divisive and so it was agreed that purely on a voluntary basis departments should agree to participate in the knowledge that there would be a payback of two hours per week for the person nominated as subject mentor, and a boost to departmental funds for materials used by the students'. A professional mentor was appointed from the senior management team. There appears to have been no animosity from the staff, who have taken five associates for a full practice with 'no problems because we realize that they are generally an asset to the school – more bodies, more ways of working, more thoughts about educational matters as we hear of what they have done in college'.

The payment system is complex to allow for the varying involvement of different schools in each term, but Churchover as a core school has an annual payment for the notional numbers in the spring term. With five full-time students, a total of £4,000 has been credited to the school. One college offers accredited INSET at a reduced rate and the school has made purchases of training against the credit accrued. The payment is also used to fund the equivalent of two lessons per week (1.10 minutes) for each subject mentor, and to allow for the incentive payment and 0.1 time for the professional mentor. There is a mentor 'feeling that this is only sufficient for the paper work which we have to do, and for the planning for the students for the coming week, but it is by no means a reward for the time we spend in debriefing and simply being a support for the student'.

The departmental additions are 'more than spent on the extra resources which the student needs – worksheets, additional texts and so on – but we know that there is some gain in the classroom itself and the department has benefited from the additions to the teaching power which can't be quantified'. It is clear that the mentors and subject staff are now questioning whether the funding is adequate for the 'training which we realize that we do, and there is a need to give the department more for its efforts – time in lieu is not a fair argument'. As more of the mentors attend meetings at one or other of the colleges, the professional mentor is aware of 'a groundswell of opinion that we may need to look at the support we are able to give the staff who, within a department, feel that they are not getting any recognition for their work'.

All arrangements are monitored by the head who has now published a proposed future structure which would build upon existing practice but would integrate the professional development and initial training work in the belief that the staff development plan could 'spot the way in which having students can help us develop skills within school, and having links with colleges can help us to develop support for staff outside the school'. Whatever the intent, all staff see the associates as 'students', although a subject teacher accepts that 'they have been into staff, parents and departmental meetings this year by invitation and we are beginning to see that they have something to offer'.

The subject mentors have been nominated by their departments. In two cases they are heads of department and carry 'the responsibility for the paper work and planning but share the supervision group by group with the staff who do the teaching'. Two are second in department but again fulfil the administrative function only. The fifth is 'a one-man band and the supervision of the associate is just something else taken on if the head wants us to be part of the scheme'. The mentors do see advantages in participation but tend to 'see it for the department rather than for myself – I had not really thought that there might be some career opportunity as a result of what I am doing – I suppose that it could be a help on the cv'. The professional mentor believes that the work will be 'helpful in proving that I can bring administration and professional development together when it comes to my next application – I would like to look at promotion and this may well have been of great help'.

There is some concern that, in a relatively small school, the impact of associates may be too great. In order to monitor this, the deputy head maintains an annual audit of contact across the year groups, and also longitudinally so that impact over a period of time is recognized. However, mentors argue that 'the way we are now approaching teacher training is such that it is a matter of the associate working alongside staff and then staff monitoring the associate so closely that the pupils only see that they have two teachers for a period of the year – it wouldn't have worked on the old pattern and our parents would have been very anxious to avoid it'. The constant supervision of teaching situations by the mentors ensures that there are no individual tensions and this is 'one of the greatest gains from the change of system – the pupils are not given the opportunity to create chaos'.

The professional mentor believes that the mentoring role 'has just grown within the limitations imposed by the HEI contracts'. The practice varies from department to department but the timetable is usually by agreement once the 'target groups' have been defined. The proposals are checked with the deputy head and professional mentor in line with the contact audit, and the completion of lesson observations on a weekly basis for each group taught is undertaken by the 'host' teacher. The professional development profiles are completed either by the subject mentor or the teacher concerned with a particular group, and final reports are prepared by the subject mentor and the professional mentor together. Counselling is usually a matter for the 'member of staff that the student gets along best with' and college links are managed by the subject mentor and professional mentor acting together. The professional mentor comments that: 'It has not been a matter so much of negotiation as of evolution of a way of working which reflected the best practice at the time'.

The staff concerned are aware that the new role has brought with it the development of some new skills. One commented that 'to be able to shut yourself off from all the other worries for an hour or so each week requires time management, but also the ability to share in the process of evaluation and reflection – it is the first time in many years that I have been forced into thinking not only about what the associate is doing but also what it lets me know about myself'. Initial mentor training, shared by the whole staff, revealed 'the need to stand back and think, to sort out the rationale for so much that we have done on automatic, and to consider how we might best help the student – it was more than how to use the materials the colleges had provided, it was more about building a bridge to the student'. The mentors have expressed the view that the first year of the new scheme was heavily concerned with 'how to do the process', the second year has been concerned with 'why we do things in certain ways and whether they are successful as teaching strategies', and 'I imagine that we shall look towards understanding the theory of learning by associates and pupils as we try to become more effective'. One mentor concludes that the skills are seen to be 'those we thought that we had developed as pastoral staff but written larger as we cope with the personal needs of people who are undergoing a good deal of stress'.

The potential tie between professional development and teacher education has resulted in an attempt to analyse training needs identified in appraisal in terms of pedagogic development within the initial training framework. 'Where a member of staff feels the need to develop a particular skill, eg, in counselling, we can provide some help through the mentor training, and where we see a group of people who want to develop a particular theme, such as effective observation, we can pull upon the staff in college A; college B is less able to help but does its best on a one-to-one basis'. The view has been expressed that some of the HEI staff should be available as a prop within the school during parts of the training year, but the reallocation of duties within this sector of higher education has minimized the opportunities for this.

The mentors appear to be motivated by the advantages of having 'additional interested and capable teachers working alongside us in the department'. One mentor comments that, 'the first time I did it I thought that it was going to be a chore, but I have been lucky and gained from watching a young and keen individual gain in competence and confidence and I know that because we have worked with Joanne we have thought about our approaches to the start and finish of lessons for example – we may have slipped into bad habits and the expectations of showing nothing but the best to an associate keeps us all alive!' The mentors were aware that the problems of a weak associate could militate against enjoyment, but they feel that the support of professional mentor and college would counter any difficulties. They see the problems as being much more related to handling hostile relationships rather than incompetence.

The control within the institution is firmly in the hands of the subject mentors and the professional mentor with line management responsibility via the deputy head to the head, but the professional mentor stresses that 'things don't really work that way in such a small school and we tend to get the people concerned together and talk it over'. There is a consistent approach between departments with broadly similar expectations for students to attend weekly meetings with their mentors and a discussion session with the professional mentor. Conflict is limited, but it 'may be that the degree of care given in one department may not be matched within a different subject area'. There is also potential conflict 'in expectations where the mentor is a busy head of department and does not give the role the priority that others feel is necessary'. Overall the staff view is that they are doing what was wanted by the head, and after some probing one mentor admitted 'that we went into the arrangement because there was no alternative and some of us see the associates as another chore – they may not always get the help which the missionaries are prepared to give'. In practical terms, the associates have also expressed the view that within this school there have been limited cross-curricular opportunities because of the strongly departmental control of arrangements.

The direct benefits to the school are limited because of the very 'high cost in time and in the planning needed during the initial phases – it may be that things will improve and I certainly feel that I can do better for both the associates'. The costs of having the associates are met in terms of administration, resources and so on, but there is 'a hidden cost in that each of the departments concerned has to spend time helping a new member of the team into the place'. The time taken with induction at a busy stage at either the beginning or end of term is stressed, and mentors are also aware of the additional training needs which wouldn't exist if the associates were not present. At the same time, one comments that 'there is some gain because we are all on the ball as far as our own standards are concerned and we do have the advantages of sharing with associates who bring newer ideas from their own subject courses, and we get another pair of hands in so many teaching situations'. The professional mentor reflects the view of mentors that there is 'little gain in the time that we are allegedly freed because the observation and debriefing takes as long if not longer, and the talk of a summer term payback seems to be illusory because the associates are going to need help with a cross-curricular approach which will demand more of us, although I suspect that the quality of what is achieved will do something for the resources and the approaches we use with the pupils in later work'. To the associate the system is perceived as 'giving great benefits – we have the advantages of being one of a group with mutual support and the chance of letting off steam without it causing nuclear fallout, and at the same time being part of a well-organized practice with a great deal of support'. There are times when associates question 'whether the staff really do want us here, although I have enjoyed my practice'. The staff as a whole have accepted the new arrangements because so many of them are involved in the process, but there are 'some domestic pressures – staff accommodation, work space, people in the laboratory, other demands on the administration and technical support, the need to help others do jobs which it would be quicker to do yourself...and the pressure on established relationships, but that said, we do gain on balance and there is a certain status in being thought worthy of supporting the work'.

The change of attitude to teacher education has been achieved because the head has attempted to show the staff that the link can be used to support so much professional development work to the advantage of individual staff within the school. The introduction was perceived by staff to have been achieved 'in the usual way by the head making a presentation to the heads of department, and then, after listening to them, to the staff as a whole and seeking opinion before a decision is taken – it usually means that we follow because it is her job to carry us forward'. There has been no adverse reaction except to one associate on personal grounds, but the professional mentor feels that 'this hasn't altered the basic view that this is a good scheme and that we are gaining from so much that the colleges are putting our way'.

## Case Study D: Highfield

### Imposed participation. Disparate management

*This case study shows how varying staff perceptions, and a 'bolt-on' organization, lead to a lack of consistency in the provision of training opportunities for associates. This does not mean that associates are not having good teacher education, but this is more dependent upon the relationship with individual mentors than with a supportive organization.*

In 1992 the HEI approached the school with a request that it should be a partner in the new arrangements. The then head was opposed to any further commitment on the grounds that 'it might interfere even more with the timetable arrangements for the pupils, it will lead to problems with apportioning the money and it could lead staff into doing work for which they have neither the time nor the skills'. He retired early in the academic year and his acting successor was prepared, after pressure from the professional mentor and the HEI, to consider a change of policy. This was achieved by discussion between the senior staff group, and then consultation with the heads of department. The reasoning was variously given that 'it might help to be associated with a major new development especially if it was going to become part of policy in the future', 'it might allow the pupils some additional classroom input which would help with differentiated work', 'it might bring about some refreshing approaches from young people who have new ideas', and it 'has some value for INSET work for the staff concerned'. The acting head felt that the only requirement was 'that we should be in control'. There was some discussion of the financial arrangements but the professional mentor felt that 'these were never, and given the limitation on funds, never could be an inducement'.

The decision to participate was taken by the senior management team and the heads of department, and the professional mentor believes that 'there was no way in which the staff as a whole were involved in the discussion, although when the announcement was made that we would be taking associates it was agreed that individual staff would retain the right to say "no" – in short it was a negative let out rather than a positive welcome for the new operation – indeed I don't think the staff as a whole realize that anything has changed'.

The management structures of the school were subject to change with the appointment of a new head, but although the professional development work for the staff is realized, there is 'no readiness on the part of senior management to integrate the mentoring role with that of staff development'. The deputy head summarizes the current view, 'that the relationships with the HEI are good and we are able to make things work with the present plans whereby the staff concerned take on additional responsibilities outside the overall management pattern and objectives of the school'. All final policy decisions are made by the deputy head with the professional mentor – there is no link to the other aspects of professional development work within the school.

The allocation of income is such that 15 per cent is added to the central funds to 'benefit the school as a whole for taking the associates', 0.1 staffing is paid for to allow the professional mentor to run the training with four free periods per week, and the remaining income is divided between the subject mentors on a contract basis with an allocation of 11 hours in the first term, 5 hours in the second term and five hours in the third term for each pair or single student according to the term. The resultant payment is £24 per hour. The school makes no allowance of time for the mentoring process 'which one mentor says is alright whilst the associates are able to meet up with us after school, but those who live at a distance have had problems'.

The subject mentors meet with the professional tutor at half-termly intervals. This work is not given either time allocation or funding and usually 'takes place over a beer and a sandwich in the pub at lunch-time'. However, the meetings are 'a real opportunity to coordinate what we are doing, to communicate with the HEI through S, the professional mentor, and to plan the activities at minimum cost to the pupils'. There is a general policy that limits pupil exposure to associates to once per group per year, although the setting arrangements do make this difficult in one year group. In English and science, associates take all ability and age groups 'because they will be on their own at the end of the block practice and we cannot deny them the opportunity to meet all sorts of teaching situations', and 'because they are capable of giving at all stages and we don't have to be too protective of our pupils; after all we are not paragons of virtue'. An opposing view is expressed in maths where 'we are taking too much of a risk by exposing the pupils to students at this stage – so much depends on the examination results, and we have to think of the way in which the public see what we do'. Further discussion with this member of staff indicated that there is a tension between her and the head of department and that she was following the departmental view unwillingly. There is evidence that the associate within this department has not had a happy or particularly helpful practice.

There is a policy agreement that the bulk of the teaching should be with groups normally taught by the mentor. Indeed, this is suggested as the opportunity for the staff concerned to gain some time 'whilst the students are taking their groups', but the mentors all have continuing involvement with their groups. In science this is 'because we need to come and go through the rooms and in so doing I can keep an eye on what is happening – there are times when the student and I team teach, either to support him or to enable us to do something with different groups'. In English the progression from 'work with individuals through work with groups to full class teaching within the first three weeks has given the classes a view that either of us will be functioning at any time – the kids get a much better programme as a result and the opportunities for effective monitoring are increased'. In maths the protection required for all groups results in a combination of team teaching and in supervised activity 'which', the associate comments, 'I don't altogether like but there are signs that I am left on my own increasingly'. The view of the senior management team is that they are prepared to accommodate the HEI until 'the stage where the parents start to make observations which could be detrimental when you consider how we are in such open competition'.

The mentors 'got there by being in a situation where I was willing to help' and 'by using my gut reaction after 23 years of teaching'. The invitation to mentor came from the professional tutor after discussion with heads of department. In one department other staff have become involved to the extent that departmental meetings involve some discussion of approaches to mentoring, but this may be because the teaching timetable for the student spans several groups taught by different colleagues. There is no feeling that the school should be seeking replacement mentors because 'the responsibility for all that must rest with the HEI, and if we have students in any subject in any one year then we need to negotiate to see how we can meet requests'. This view ties in with the management detachment from the mentoring process.

The training for mentors to ensure coherence in the experience does not appear to be meeting its objective, as shown in the departmental variation. Maths has a profile completion session by negotiation every three weeks; science achieves completion by the mentor who then asks the associate for his observations; and the English pattern is one of negotiated completion based upon the analysis of observed lessons and the file of lesson critiques. The professional tutor 'aims to see each student once per fortnight and then to use the data to verify the professional development profile and to set targets in an appraisal fashion to match the newer experiences in staff development'. The three mentors have differing training needs largely related to the interpretation of competences according to their subject – and current HEI opportunities do not provide for this. The divergence is shown in the following mentor comment: 'There is a need to see how the associates learn about mathematical processes – we imagine that they are working as we have done after 20 years on the job!' (maths). 'I would like time to share the experiences of mentoring with other mentors – each associate is different and we need to build up a set of strategies for the differing situations' (English). 'We need to build up ways of dealing with the lack of basic knowledge when students are faced with integrated science' (science).

Of the three mentors, only one had considered the role as a possible help in promotion. The professional tutor had, however, clear career objectives: 'As head of a minor department I need to be able to offer something else in the promotion stakes – this job requires working with people, administrative work and a lot of negotiation – the trouble is that few of the hierarchy realize this!' The present organization of the school does not allow for the role to be other than an extra function where the member of staff acts as an agency in the same way as an examiner and, in the circumstances, 'there is little hope that it will ever be part of the promotion structure here'.

The motivation for the four staff concerned appears to lie entirely in their enjoyment of the work. 'The total income for the term will be £124 less tax, NI – it's a laugh really and there is no more in it than a meal out, but I do enjoy the opportunity of sharing what I do with the young people – they give a lot, and they also make me think about my work – maybe that gives my kids a better sort of teacher'. For the professional mentor, 'I certainly am not in it for the money – that is not the attraction – it is something about sharing my enjoyment with people who are usually appreciative'. The mentors all mentioned that other staff speak of the time relief they get and that this was in no way a motivating factor because 'we have to spend so much more time out of the lesson – it makes it ludicrous to suggest that we are doing it for the time it gives us'. There is a camaraderie between the subject mentors 'born of our need to make ourselves a force in the land', and the fact that the meetings are held in a local pub to enhance the social atmosphere, but 'this does further marginalize something which the senior staff see as an added extra anyway'.

The professional mentor believes that if he is to get the time to make the system work effectively, he will have to talk directly to the head 'because there is nobody else who takes policy responsibility – it's almost a tack on to the organization of the school'. There have been two areas of tension in the past term. In maths the need to spread the associate across the work of several colleagues has had an implied problem arising 'from the need to know who the mentor is, and from the fact that the named mentor is then doing the follow-up from other people's work'. In all subjects there have been tensions when the demands of the associate have conflicted with the needs of the department, eg, in attendance at meetings or in the completion of administrative tasks when the associate has had a pre-arranged meeting. The staff as a whole seem unaware that there has been a change in the way in which training is being undertaken and some find it difficult to appreciate the need for mentors. The HEI link tutor said that 'The scheme was explained at a staff meeting, but only the departments involved really bothered – there is still need for whole staff training on the change. The profile documents are not widely known and the concept of developing competencies has only been explained to the staff who work directly with the students – its potential for the staff as a whole has not yet been realized'.

It is difficult to see whether the school feels that it has gained or lost by the arrangement. In financial terms there is little to be gained by the school as a whole and 'there is an opportunity cost in all that we do – the staff concerned are tied up during a term when we might be looking for their help in extramural activities or when the examination groups need particular help'. At the same time the mentors acknowledge the opportunities for individual support, group work and 'getting on with some of the jobs which can be done whilst the students are in the classroom'. The English mentor feels that 'the students do bring the opportunity to think a bit more about what we are doing and have ideas of their own if they are good', and the professional mentor argues that 'the school gains from having extra people on site and helping on the fringe with so much that we do – if students are to have a worthwhile experience they need to be part of the place'. All three of the block practice associates have contributed to extramural activities: football, rugby, drama and music during a very busy term.

This is a school in which the care of students is by evolution rather than revolution. One of the peripheral staff is in charge of special needs and comments that 'It is only because we know what has happened in the main subjects that we know what the advantages of the new scheme might be – and we have had good associates who have been happy to share their experience with us'. There are concerns that the changed scheme will bring additional work with very little return in either time or financial reward, to the extent that some subject staff will be unwilling to participate, and there is a feeling that the involvement reflects the enthusiasm of the professional mentor rather than a wish on the part of the staff as a whole to be committed.

*Chapter 4*

# The Mentor

*Linda Devlin*

This chapter draws on the experience of the author as a mentor researcher. It presents, from a mentor's perspective, research evidence synthesized from both the mentor survey and the case studies within different partnership schemes. On the basis of the research evidence described, the chapter goes on to draw some conclusions and make some recommendations for the improvement of the practice of mentoring in initial teacher education in schools.

## Mentor Selection

The criteria for mentor selection are determined by the way school senior managers interpret the higher education institution (HEI) documentation. The professional mentor is responsible for the management of the partnership scheme within the school and is the point of liaison with the HEI. The decisions made at this level about the selection and management of the mentors are crucial to the success of the partnership. As one professional mentor commented, 'Once the contractual parameters were known' we suggested 'what mentors should do'. HEIs tend to trust the school 'in settling who will do the mentoring work'.

Significantly, this research identifies a precursory stage to mentor selection, that is, the selection of schools and subject departments, often 'on the basis of the HEIs need rather than suitability'. There are strong indications that the choice of a department within a particular school depends on whether it is 'known' to the curriculum tutors in the HEI. The decision-making process for selecting departments employs unspecified performance criteria (for example a large and or successful department) which are not explicit in any of the partnership documentation. More recently, however, the process of identifying suitable subject departments has, increasingly, become a two-way process.

Departments in schools are beginning to exercise their right to choose whether or not to be involved in training teachers.

In many cases, therefore, the critical criterion for mentor selection was the choice of department, because the head of department frequently assumed the role. The 'number of people from whom they can choose is very small, it is usually a job which has to be done and which can only be done by the number two because he or she has the length of experience it needs'. This appears to have happened in eight schools, but practice varies and some of these have no volunteers because the head of department has 'retained the reins of control because he or she feels that they are the only one to do the job'. One of this group of mentors comments that although he is a volunteer he had had to be persuaded, but 'was aware of the pressures which failure to help would put the head of department under'. Put at its highest, though, the head of department 'saw it as a career opportunity which could not be missed by the mentor and he encouraged participation', but at the other extreme, 'there was nobody else to do the job in the department'.

The survey data show that 55 per cent of mentors are heads of department and see responsibility for associates as part of their job. The interviews revealed that for some it is included in their job description. In a few departments the head of department delegated the mentor role to another member of the team. Alternatively, all the members of a department have a team responsibility with one teacher designated as 'mentor'.

In looking for mentors, either by invitation or by internal advertisement response, senior managers have specified 'some experience of teacher training', 'former involvement with the HEI scheme', 'a long period of successful teaching', 'the skills of empathy, supporting and counselling', 'an ability to cope with the administrative work and the integration of associates with the life of the school', 'an awareness of the way in which the subject should be developing' and 'a genuine interest in the work'. However, many mentors believe that there are no criteria for mentor selection and that they are involved on an ad hoc, voluntary basis. Other mentors considered selection to be vaguely based on criteria of which they were not aware. The evidence from the research indicates that 93 per cent of mentors had volunteered their involvement in the partnership. Mentors believed they had been subject to 'some sort of vague selection process' but were not able to elaborate on this other than an intuitive claim that the professional mentor and their line manager felt they were suitable and would 'do a good job'. 'The supposition that any member of staff is capable of mentoring' appeared to be generally rejected. Some mentors inherited the role or had been working with trainee teachers for many years. Their continued involvement in the changed course provision did not require reselection but it had made teachers re-evaluate the role, especially as many of them were 'middle ranking, long serving, and in need of some new challenge'. It was easy for them to be 'caught up in past practices'.

In numerous schools individuals were invited to become a mentor because they were perceived as having the 'necessary qualities'. These mentor qualities or competences are not necessarily an explicit feature of partnership documentation. In all three partnerships the requirements of the role are described in the HEI documentation and senior managers must, if adhering to contract, use these guidelines to inform the selection of mentors. The areas of competence could be summarized as the qualities of a good role model, guidance and counselling skills, monitoring and assessment skills, knowledge and experience and organizational skills.

The mentors interviewed did not believe that these guidelines had actually been used as the criteria for selection, but some of the criteria they did mention did fall into three of the areas of 'providing a good role model, offering guidance and counselling, and with strong knowledge and experience within their subject'. They were variously identified as:

Role model qualities:

- 'a suitable, adaptable, sympathetic, understanding personality';
- 'reliable, conscientious';
- 'articulate'
- had 'an interest in their own evolution'.

Guidance and counselling skills:

- 'good interpersonal skills';
- 'supportive';
- 'accessibility'.

Knowledge/experience:

- 'teaching and academic ability';
- 'philosophical grasp of mentoring';
- 'experience of teaching';
- 'experience of working with trainee teachers';
- 'interest in information technology'.

Although mentors did not identify skills and qualities in the areas of monitoring, assessment and organization as important in their selection, they are aware of a need for professional development in these areas. In the mentor survey, 100 per cent described assessment training as important and 97 per cent thought training in organization quite or very important.

The best experiences of mentor selection occurred either when school senior managers, in discussion with departmental staff, used clear criteria to select mentors, or where a deliberate effort was made to encourage members of a departmental team to undertake the mentoring role as part of their professional development. In one school, interviews were used to make the selection of the mentors. The criteria used in the interviews were not specified. Occasionally teachers with a specific interest in teacher training asked to be mentors. In two case study schools teachers were selected as mentors on this basis. However, this model can only work if the teacher's subject is offered as a course in the HEI. If not, the school will have to make arrangements with another institution or not receive any associates. This can lead to 'overload if schemes have different requirements'.

Those responsible for managing teacher training in schools, the professional mentor and the senior management team, preferred mentors to be well-established and experienced members of staff because mentoring responsibilities are 'demanding in all sorts of ways'. There are many occasions when this is not possible because workload, human frailty and the pressure of finding suitable placements, lead to the selection of an unsuitable or inexperienced teacher as a mentor which, in turn, gives rise to concerns about the quality of the associate teacher's tutelage and about the quality of learning experienced by pupils.

## Role Definition and Negotiation

Initially, the role of the mentor was defined by the HEIs, both formally in the documentation and training, and informally through the everyday workings of the partnership. The mentors' role was negotiated between the members of the partnership but it has continued to evolve over time, according to the needs and experience of individual schools. There is considerable agreement that partnership schemes, involving a large number of institutions and personnel, must have a clearly defined minimum role for mentors, in order to ensure that associate teachers are not subject to 'idiosyncratic approaches' and that they have consistency of experience. The HEIs identified the key characteristics of the mentoring role and have provided clear guidance for those involved.

Despite this guidance, some mentors still do not seem to be aware of the formalization of their role. One mentor felt that there was 'an expectation that we are good teachers and will transmit those values, but there is no attempt, as yet, to define what we should be doing'. Consequently, individual mentors adopt 'their own style'. Many considered the role to be 'flexible' and saw it as a framework 'on which mentors put a personal stamp'. It was common for mentors to think they had negotiated their role with the professional mentor within their school. One mentor acknowledged the need to be 'assessed in what I am doing because I am so much of a beginner in all this – our competences are in need of review'. 'Trying to establish shared values' is apparently perceived as an important factor in ensuring sound mentor practice. Since, in the experience of the author, HEIs do not monitor mentor practice in any formal way, this variation of view is not entirely surprising. The quality of the teacher training experience will depend to some extent on continuity and consistency of mentoring across institutions.

The formalization of the mentors' responsibilities conflicts with the informal arrangements used by mentors to set aside time to carry out their responsibilities. Time is needed for reflection, discussion, administrative demands and research. However, most schools do not allocate time within the school day for mentoring responsibilities; mentors give their own time. It was common for mentors to find themselves with 'a catalogue of disasters in keeping appointments'. Practical problems arise because a block of time is needed for discussions between the mentor and the trainee, especially in the associate's early weeks in school. The survey of mentors showed that only 33 per cent had meetings timetabled. The reality for many is that much discussion takes place at times which are inappropriate, short and spasmodic, depending, in many cases, on the concurrence of mentor and associate non-contact time. If this concurrence of non-contact time is not built into the timetable, 'the opportunity to debrief' has to be found 'when and where they can and often with a lot of pressure' before and after school. This does not always adequately meet the needs of the associate. As the associate becomes more competent, more time can be created for the mentor and appropriate consultation can take place more easily. This research showed that schools which do allocate timetabled discussion time allow one hour per week; however, 98 per cent of the mentors spend more than one hour and 14 per cent spend more than three hours (see Table 4.1).

**Table 4.1** *Weekly time spent discussing work with associate teachers*

|  | *Frequency* | *Per cent* |
| --- | --- | --- |
| Less than an hour | 2 | 2 |
| 1 to 2 hours | 54 | 54 |
| 2 to 3 hours | 30 | 30 |
| More than 3 hours | 14 | 14 |

Additionally the research ascertained that 68 per cent of mentors attended meetings at least once per term either at school or the HEI, but that 21 per cent of schools did not hold any mentor meetings. When meetings occurred, the agenda in many schools was tightly focused on administration. The data suggest that the partnership issues are not being addressed in school development plans, nor is mentoring included in the staff development plan – a reflection of the bolt-on nature of the partnership arrangements in some schools. Even where associates are apparently well integrated into the day-to-day running of the school, the management of the training is not well integrated.

## Mentor Perceptions of Associate Teachers

The overwhelming attitude to the presence of associate teachers in schools was that the 'advantages outweighed the disadvantages'. Senior managers felt that 'the environment for the whole staff was enhanced by the presence of the associate teachers'. One mentor commented on the 'intense enjoyment of the teaching situation at student and pupil level' as a result of working with associates. The research gave indications that the benefits of competent associates might include the introduction of:

- 'new teaching and learning styles, for example team teaching';
- 'new ideas for enhancing pupil learning or a fresh approach to the work of the department';
- 'additional classroom input which would help with differentiated work';
- 'change in the work and vision of a department';
- 'improved pupil/teacher ratios';
- 'help for reading, duty support, registration and the development of activity workshops';
- 'better assessment of pupils, preparation of displays, preparation of schemes of work, development of learning materials and a contribution to pastoral and counselling roles';
- 'increased extracurricular activities' such as 'work with drama, guitars and chess'.

In addition to the formal, contractual responsibilities depicted thus far, there are a number of equally important informal socio-cultural responsibilities concerned with the enhancement of associate status and with the creation of a positive image of all associates in the eyes of pupils and their parents. When the associates are treated as, and perceived to be, members of staff, the environment created will enrich the teaching in the school. The difficulty is that many teachers are still unaccustomed or uneasy with the presence of other adults in their classrooms, but this will become a necessity in the current climate where mentoring, appraisal and more regular school inspections have a high profile. It is also important for the management of the school, including the governors, to recognize the associates as an integral part of the life of the school; to ensure that, as one senior manager explained, 'we are gaining prestige from the involvement' and there it is a positive experience for the staff as a whole.

## Effects on Pupils

Mentors are ambivalent about the effect of school-based teacher training on pupils. There were concerns about the risks of 'exposing the pupils to students' because 'so much depends on examination results'; on the other hand, mentors did not want to be 'too protective' of their pupils. Teachers appreciate the dangers of exposing pupils to 'trainee overload', particularly in small schools. Senior managers were concerned that the pupils might eventually reach 'saturation point' when their learning and motivation could be affected by contact with too great a variety of teachers. The need to control the amount of pupil contact with associate teachers was recognized by senior managers and mentors. The exclusion of some examination classes or 'difficult' groups from associate timetables was one method adopted by mentors to 'protect' pupils and associates. There was also the recognition that, no matter how good the associate, there needed to be an 'equal balance for the pupils' between having their usual class teachers and associates.

There is, at present, little evident formal monitoring of the influence of exposure to associates on pupils across the school. Occasionally, professional mentors and some departments monitored the influence of associate teachers on pupils' performance across teaching groups and classes. Many mentors would like this type of 'contact audit', used as a means of effective monitoring, to be given greater prominence, because they feel that they 'cannot let having teachers in training get in the way of clients' [needs]'. It was accepted that training teachers must not 'interfere with the daily work of the school or impact adversely upon the pupils' because 'the first duty is to our pupils and parents' who are 'quick to let us know when there are problems' because parents realize that 'they are now the paymasters'.

## Skill Identification, Development and Training Needs

The research indicates that teachers consider the skills for mentoring to be similar to those learned through other aspects of the teachers' job. There was acceptance that there should 'be a very high degree of professional competence amongst the staff'. Some mentors were aware that HEIs had identified the skills required and had outlined them, in some format, in the mentoring documentation. Other teachers were unaware of the documentation, but considered themselves to already have 'all of the skills required for mentoring'. However, many acknowledged that there was a 'skills gap', and that this gap could be addressed through involvement with the partnership and through the training provided as a result of this involvement. However, training was perceived to be 'predominantly in the interests of HEI'.

The training needs of mentors fell into three categories: initial training, continuing support and professional development. These needs were being met through training days, curriculum meetings and in school support. In the 'early days of the partnership scheme, training was provided for all mentors by the HEI'. This training focused, in line with the requirements of the HEI, on the administrative structures which were being developed and on supplying examples of 'good mentoring practice'. This induction was seen by mentors as a valuable experience which tied in 'with other aspects of staff development' and helped 'their understanding of the management of educational processes'. Mentors recognized that training had to move away from organization and administration towards a more innovative, pedagogical role, within their subject area. However, the training currently provided by HEI curriculum tutors was described as 'not well structured' with much 'variation between curriculum areas within the same partnership scheme'. Mentors indicated that important areas of skills training outside their subject specialisms were time management, observation, counselling and debriefing and for a few, information technology skills.

Few mentors acknowledged any benefit of mentor training to their other school responsibilities. One mentor noted an 'overall improvement in personal teaching standards with improved lesson structure' and greater 'awareness of the classroom situation' which they saw leading to improvement in the 'accuracy' of their teaching. Mentors have become more reflective about their own practice and are more concerned with the reappraisal aspects of their own teaching. Some recognized the similarities to the skills required for appraisal and other aspects of staff development. In order to meet the needs of the individual mentors and schools, at a local level, training is now provided directly or indirectly through the school staff development programme. Two schools were building the mentor training into a whole school approach to staff development on the lines of Investors in People. Seventy-nine per cent of mentors who responded to the survey agreed that the mentoring skills acquired through the partnership were valued as a development opportunity, but they did not see the role as 'either permanent or a key to the future'. Some felt that they were responsible for defining their own training needs and that the university did not always respond to these needs.

In an attempt to assess the needs of mentors for future training, we asked respondents to evaluate their perceived ability and experience as part of the mentoring culture within their schools. This self-assessment, shown in Table 4.2, was then investigated further in an attempt to ascertain specific training needs. The overwhelming training need appears to be associated with a feeling on the part of mentors that they lack the necessary information and knowledge for their pedagogic, rather than their subject-based task. This reflects the comparatively early stage of development of the mentoring scheme, the lack of certainty about the school role in undertaking work previously seen as the responsibility of the HEI, and the organizational rather than philosophical emphasis of mentor training to date. However, more detailed investigation suggests that within each functional area there are strengths and weaknesses.

**Table 4.2** *Mentors' functional self-assessment*

| Function | Able and experienced % | Need more experience % | Not confident % |
| --- | --- | --- | --- |
| Role model as teacher | 87 | 13 | – |
| Advisor/counsellor | 78 | 20 | 2 |
| Monitoring/assessment | 71 | 24 | 5 |
| Knowledge/information | 36 | 48 | 12 |
| Course tutor in school | 51 | 31 | 16 |

The role model is believed to be attained in developing good pupil-teacher relationships (85 per cent), the establishment of good working relationships with colleagues (80 per cent), the identification and demonstration of good practice (78 per cent) and the use of a variety of teaching methods (73 per cent). Mentors express reservations about their effective deployment of communication skills (62 per cent), their ability to demonstrate good organization and administration (61 per cent), and the development of personal time management skills (52 per cent). Interview evidence suggests that the latter may result from the heavy burden of other administrative demands upon mentors: 'I feel that so much of the time the associate must see an example of some-body under pressure with snatched discussion here and there – but school life is like that unless you are in the classroom'.

The only attribute which was believed to be possessed by less than half the mentors (42 per cent) was the ability to engage in self-assess-ment and evaluation – possibly also a reflection of 'the pressures we are under', but an indication of necessary skills training either within the schools or the HEI.

As advisor and counsellor, the ability to help associates in the prepa-ration of lesson plans was rated most highly at 80 per cent, but the abil-ity and experience to cope drop markedly in matters of support for associates with personal difficulties (61 per cent), confidence building (65 per cent) and the ability to represent the interests of associates with other staff (58 per cent). Training needs appear to be greatest in matters of self-evaluation (51 per cent), and career development for the associates (44 per cent). Again, this requires the development of skills and understanding which were previously the accepted role of the HEI.

The need for further training in monitoring and assessment showed the importance of pedagogic awareness. Only 68 per cent of the cohort felt that they were able and experienced in lesson observation, and 62 per cent felt that they were giving effective feedback, with 52 per cent of the mentors feeling comfortable with the feedback given to associates. Perceived needs included the development of appropriate assessment information (only 38 per cent of mentors believed that they were competent and experienced in this), and of the approach to the completion of the associates' personal profile and teaching file (32 per cent). This evidence supports an expressed view that 'the whole train-ing programme is at a very early stage of development...we seem to know about administrative procedures but we haven't yet had the time or the opportunity to work through the deeper issues of assessment with colleagues across the partnership'.

In the provision of appropriate information, while there was a gener-ally good evaluation of the ability to provide knowledge of the resources available (84 per cent), and of subject development (71 per cent), and of the school as an organization (70 per cent), there was considerable concern at the perceived inability to provide information on subject-based developments in other schools (26 per cent), and, most importantly, on the requirements for attainment of the CATE competences. In short, mentors felt 'that we need to know what it is that the HEI used to teach and what we are now expected to explore in theoretical terms...and we just haven't had the training or experience to make that readily available'.

The lack of theoretical understanding also underpins responses concerning the role of the mentor as a course tutor for the PGCE in the school. While there is some confidence in the ability to demonstrate good pupil management skills (75 per cent), and some ability and experience in coping with record keeping and reporting (62 per cent) and issues of professionalism (59 per cent), there is a need for training in adolescent development (34 per cent), in demonstrating the theories of learning (31 per cent), and in explaining the relevance of the psychological and sociological background to education to associates. Again, the latter elements are seen as the work of the HEI: 'They seem to have landed the lot on us and we all suffer from chronic amateurism in meeting the needs of quick associates who spot our ineptitude'.

Two of the three HEIs have already moved towards the provision of a Certificate in Mentoring which is designed to provide the necessary knowledge, experience and time for reflection needed to increase the competences required. The third HEI is proposing to offer the work as part of an MA programme, but the dilemma remains that 'until it is a requirement of every mentor, we cannot be sure that they will have had the necessary training, and if we demand that mentors undertake the training, then we shall never get the volunteers we want' (head).

Information technology (IT) was considered to be a strength of the training in some schools. A few schools with adequate facilities provided short introductory courses for all associates during the early weeks of the course. Unfortunately, in most schools IT was considered to be inadequate because schools do not have the facilities to guarantee IT training across all curriculum areas. Many mentors do not have appropriate IT skills and schools have a great variety of IT provision. Some mentors were not aware of the need for experience in this area. Access to and use of IT in teaching programmes varied considerably from subject to subject within each school. Often the mentors were learning from the associates. The level of trainee competence was the critical factor in determining IT use during their time in school.

## Career Expectations of Mentors

Mentoring is seen by most mentors as a positive contribution to an individual's career profile, although some mentors had 'not yet grasped the developmental implications of their work'. Where the mentor was a head of department, 'mentoring' was commonly seen as a duty. Senior managers did not always appreciate the significant benefit of the role of mentor to the career profile of an individual. It was credited as a worthwhile method of self-evaluation and little more. However, enlightened senior managers were quick to discern mentoring as an appropriate means of 'career enrichment' and stated that 'the role has some career enhancement prospects'. The value of mentoring 'to future career moves would depend on the post that an individual was applying for'. Senior managers felt that all staff benefit 'through professional development, INSET or other staff training' because of the whole school involvement in the partnership. One senior manager commented, 'we are aware of the change it has brought to people and would certainly look at involvement when interviewing new staff'.

Seventy-nine per cent of mentors, mainly women and the professional mentors, think of mentoring in terms of personal development. Some individuals specified clear career goals such as 'ambitions to work in HE' as an education or curriculum tutor or to work in the schools as 'teacher in charge of teacher training'. Others hoped that they would be 'able to offer something else in the promotion stakes' in order to find 'a way forward which involves the subject and my enthusiasm for working with the transmission of ideas to others'. Some mentors were concerned that when mentoring was used in job applications it would not be valued by other schools, particularly if they were not involved in teacher training. This was reinforced by a senior manager who said mentoring 'is just not at that level in the order of priorities'.

Mentors felt that training and experience should be formalized and recognized by an accredited training system and qualification. Mentors are already taking advantage of the opportunities offered on a variety of training schemes which lead to additional qualifications at certificate, diploma and masters level. Two of the HEIs involved in the partnership schemes with the case study schools offer training discounts for partnership schools. Senior managers in some schools are eager to ensure 'that we get the best possible deal in a complex but integrated system where investment in people is given priority'. Important links were seen to exist between training teachers and other aspects of professional development, particularly if it was 'at no cost, except in time, but to our mutual benefit if we integrate it with the professional development work'.

An additional benefit, in schools where a large percentage of the staff had many years of service in the school, was that 'a sudden influx of younger professionals enlivened the staff'. Many of the staff welcomed 'a bit more time, a bit more cash and a bit more flexibility' that having associates in the school created. Senior managers, mentors and the associates all emphasized the importance of the academic element of the training courses provided by the HEIs. This academic link not only benefited the associates, it was also perceived to be a benefit to the school as a whole. A further whole school benefit was that 'working with new teachers had improved the cooperation among the staff'.

## Motivation

A key motivational aspect of mentoring was its contribution to a new generation of the teaching profession. The idea of 'giving something back to the profession' or 'sharing experience' was regularly put forward as a reason for involvement. Many teachers were conscious that having associates in school had generated enthusiasm in their subject area and helped mentors themselves to reflect on practice in providing 'a challenge, camaraderie and personal learning'. In some small departments there was the added advantage of working closely with an enthusiastic colleague who 'shared common interests and expertise in a subject'.

Although 49 per cent of mentors in the survey cohort are paid for their responsibilities in the partnership, there was considerable agreement amongst mentors that motivation was not in any way linked with financial remuneration. Initially teachers became involved when there was no financial incentive and even now mentors are fully aware that the time and effort involved are only partly compensated for by financial gain.

A further motivational aspect for many mentors was the sense of being in a partnership which was seen as a healthy working relationship that created conscientious professionals and was 'value for money' to the associates. A common expression was that the associates must be getting value for money because the experience they gained in the schools was 'priceless'. It was felt that the value for money to the school varied from year to year as a result of a number of variables which include:

- 'the quality of the associates';
- 'the willingness of the associates to involve themselves in all aspects of school life';
- 'the response of the staff involved as mentors';
- 'the pressures on the whole staff, for example, staff absence, work-load or whole school issues'.

In terms of motivation, the value to the school was that mentors were, as a result of the 'need to stand back and think', 'keeping abreast of what was happening in education and training' and sharing 'the process of evaluation and reflection' so that a 'rationale for so much that we have done on automatic' can be forged in order to 'consider how we might best help the student'.

## Tensions

Conflict is inevitable between the demands of the school and its pupils and the demands of the partnership and the trainee teachers. The main tensions with regard to the mentor's role were related to: the funding, the division of responsibilities, the increased workload, the assessment of associates and the quality of the course.

A particular funding issue in the case study schools was that 50 per cent of mentors were unpaid. This was because some senior managers 'took the position that mentors should not be paid for doing their job'. HEI have little influence over the distribution of funding once it has been allocated to schools; 'Departmental gains are small but significant'. However, there were 'hidden' costs when departments were forced to 'spend time helping a new member of the team into the place'. There is also concern in schools about the perceived 'financial top-slicing by the HEI', especially when schools are taking the major responsibility for the associates.

The funding issues, in association with the division of responsibility, disturbed mentors. They lacked confidence in the HEI support system because curriculum tutors didn't seem to 'know where they stood in the new arrangements'. Generally mentors valued the HEI link which they felt placed them 'at the forefront of training' because it linked them 'with the subject tutors who have time for research' on pedagogic processes. However, it was observed that curriculum tutors 'no longer observe lessons or make contact' and seem to have 'handed the job back at a knock down price'. Schools are reluctant to take the 'ultimate responsibility for the operation of the course' because they do not feel that this was their principal role.

Increased workload is an issue for all mentors, but it is exacerbated when the associate is not of a high calibre. One mentor commented that 'to have your own shadow for whom you are totally responsible...is a drain on mental and emotional energy'. It is possible for a department to be completely taken over by associates and for the mentor to become a colleague working in a team. At the other extreme, when an associate requires the mentor's full support throughout their school placement, there is a great increase in the workload of the mentor, the department and the school. A typical associate requires considerable mentor support in their initial period in school, but this need for support usually wanes as the associate becomes more confident and experienced until, in the case of the best associates, the mentor would benefit in a variety of ways from the associate. In addition to the personal attention required by associates, there are the 'domestic pressures – staff accommodation, work space...administration and technical support...the need to help others do jobs which it would be quicker to do yourself...and the pressure on established relationships'.

The assessment of associates was a burden to mentors who felt ill-equipped without HEI support 'to discuss fully the associates' strengths and weaknesses' and were concerned about 'the standards of pass and fail between departments and between schools'. Assessment became an important issue if the associate was borderline. Mentors believed they would 'carry the can' if the HEI did not agree with their assessment.

The quality of the course was thought by some to be at risk if a mentor 'does not give the role the priority that others feel is necessary'. It 'may be that the degree of care given in one department may not be matched within a different subject area' and this would be to the detriment of the associate.

## Policy Implications

The overwhelming opinion about mentoring was that 'staff are involved on a voluntary basis' and that individuals did not feel 'either obliged to accept the offer of becoming a mentor or feel under pressure to continue being a mentor'. Mentors believed they had a choice and it was apparent, from a range of comments made in interviews, that this has ensured that mentoring is 'undertaken by people with a commitment' to the task.

The recognition, in the research, that the selection of placements in subject departments has a significant impact on the subsequent selection of mentors emphasizes the need to define suitable criteria for the identification of schools and departments. If these criteria are not explicit, as more schools become involved and more places are required, then HEI may reach the point when the only criterion is 'will this school take trainee teachers?' In the present circumstances, as the demand for placements continues to grow, it is possible that the process will become 'demand-led rather than quality-led'.

HEIs seem reluctant to formalize explicit criteria for the selection of mentors, but they do outline the role they must play in partnership schemes. The criteria for the selection of mentors are still evolving. They are being defined and refined by the partners in an experiential way. However, where the criteria are made explicit and they are used by schools, there is greater consistency both in terms of who is involved in the selection process and about how mentors are selected, thus inevitably reducing inconsistencies in mentor practice in partnership schemes.

The research evidence indicated a degree of ambiguity in the perceptions and attitudes of mentors to their role in relation to their responsibilities and their relationships with HEI curriculum tutors. Some mentors acknowledged that the HEI guidance covered in detail mentor responsibilities, but many mentors seemed unaware of the existence of these guidelines. Mentors commented that much of the work is based on their own 'gut reaction' and although they felt competent in the role, they found difficulty defining it. Communication of the partnership processes to mentors is an essential part of the management of the scheme. Where schemes were effective in this matter, documentation given to mentors was reinforced in a number of ways through everyday practice and in support and training.

The relationship between the schools and HEIs was viewed, by the research population, with a mixture of enthusiasm and caution. In several of the case study schools there was general agreement among mentors about the aims of the partnership. Furthermore, in schools where 'mentors see themselves as part of a team whose views are sought on the management of the scheme' there is a greater sense of 'ownership and involvement' where 'a genuine sense of consensus and collegiality' develops from the opportunity to discuss 'even the most contentious of issues openly'. Where a team approach was adopted, mentors gained the advantage of a 'broader perspective' on the partnership arrangements. A further consideration is that, in some schools, many of the responsibilities of the professional mentor were delegated to the mentors so it was even more essential that they had a good working knowledge of the partnership. Where this consensus is not achieved, there was inconsistency in the type of mentor support received by the associate teachers.

In schools where the partnership structures are not well understood and mentor meetings are a rarity, the response to the HEI is more cautious. Mentors pointed out that 'there is a need for a new understanding on both sides' and that the use of mentors 'is not a cheap way of having someone else to do your work for you'. These points were essentially concerned with the role of the curriculum tutor and the supervision of associates during their time in schools. Mentors did not always feel competent to undertake all of the responsibilities which were required of them and were looking to the traditional sources of support within the HEI. Where HEIs have established a system for monitoring partnership schools for 'conformity and consistency of practice' and are offering appropriate support, 'idiosyncratic approaches' to mentoring and concerns about the impact of teacher training on standards of achievement and quality of learning are reduced.

The predominant view in the case study schools was that involvement in the partnership was advantageous to all staff and pupils. Many mentors consider that 'departmental gains are small but significant', despite the great pressures of involvement. However, little attempt is being made to assess the precise nature of these benefits. What is clear is that the range of responsibilities that the professional and teacher mentor have for the trainees is increasing as partnership schemes develop. Not all teacher mentors were aware of the full implications of these growing responsibilities.

This approach to teacher training appears more successful where associates were introduced and their role explained to pupils and parents in a way which made everyone feel comfortable about changes of teaching staff. A positive image for the associates is essential if there is to be minimum disruption and quality of learning for pupils. There is still a concern about the impact on pupils, and this needs to be assessed in all schools in a systematic way. An essential part of the management of the partnership is a 'contact audit' to monitor the impact of trainee teachers on pupil performance in particular groups, years or departments.

Mentors acknowledged a need for further training in order to bridge the 'skills gap' which many had identified in the interviews. Where schools offered mentors a range of training activities which reinforce the university approach, consistency of quality, methods and content were achieved in supporting the associates. Mentors were adamant that their training must not deteriorate into a 'twilight' gathering, consisting of a spurious package of administration, information giving and the informal anecdotal 'exchange of views'. Investment in mentor training is a benefit to the profession as a whole because it contributes to training in the future by being at the forefront in meeting the demands of national training targets.

When new mentors are appointed, the greatest advantages are apparently derived from induction which is provided by the school with the support of the HEI. There are considerable benefits where the knowledge and skills acquired from mentor training are seen as transferable to other aspects of professional development in schools, such as appraisal and the induction of new staff. Mentoring has also helped individuals to identify their own training needs which do not always fit neatly into the perception of the skills required. A particular example of this is the need for skills in information technology, which a number of mentors felt was an area where they were not confidently supporting the associate. Some mentors had benefited from the skills of the associates and had requested IT training to enhance other aspects of their work.

Mentors valued the esteem generated by their involvement with the HEI and some felt that their career profile had been enhanced by involvement in the partnership. When partnership structures are explicit in the HEI documentation and are reinforced in training, mentors are more likely to take advantage of the opportunities offered by the HEI. These may include input into the university-based elements of the course, professional education through higher degrees, involvement in practitioner research or representation of mentor views in management groups. In this situation, motivation of teachers is enhanced because they are making a major contribution to the newcomers to their profession.

Where individuals see mentoring as part of their job description or 'something else that they are required to do in a long list of responsibilities', they do not tend to consider it to be of value to them. This tends to be the case when the training of teachers is not well integrated into the management structures of the school. There is some evidence to suggest that if the mentor training is recognized by a formally accredited qualification, the mentors' motivation and participation in training is enhanced. If mentoring is to be accredited, a national scheme with clear specification of mentor knowledge and competence must be established.

In all partnership schemes where a number of different institutions with their own set of aims and priorities are working together, there are inevitably some tensions. Most of the tensions identified by mentors in the interviews are the result of poor communication of decisions in which representatives from HEIs and schools have been involved. Although a minority of school representatives contribute to partnership decision making at the strategic and tactical levels, there is clear evidence from the interviews that mentors would like a greater influence at the strategic level, which is currently dominated by HEIs. One mentor grumbled that 'important decisions were taken behind closed doors and far above the level of mentors, professional mentors and senior managers in schools'. A view prevailed that the HEIs had 'all of the power but none of the responsibility'. The main opportunity for most mentors to discuss partnership issues was at the operational level through meetings with the curriculum tutors from HEIs.

The research indicates that mentoring, at best, is a regenerating experience creating a 'feeling of worth and self-esteem'. This is because the contribution of the mentor is recognized, even though at times it is 'exhausting'. Where this is the experience of the mentor, there are 'small but significant' gains for all elements of the partnership. At worst, mentoring can be a 'burden' in a situation where a mentor has a range of responsibilities in which mentoring has a low priority. The attitude that 'we can't let having teachers in training get in the way of what the clients want' may prevail in schools where a mentoring culture is not well developed. Ultimately, mentors felt that school-based teacher training presents 'challenging opportunities' which are of significant value to pupils, associates, teachers and schools.

Chapter 5

# The Professional Mentor

*Michael Johnson*

## Introduction

In the HEI/school partnership model of initial teacher education (ITE), the term 'professional mentor' is used to identify the person in each of the partnership schools who is responsible for developing and maintaining links with the HEI, for the management of ITE in the school and usually for the provision of the school-based programme of study concerned with whole school and cross-curricular issues. It is clear from the evidence of our research that in the HEI/school partnership model of ITE, the role of the professional mentor is of crucial importance for the organization and administration of the school attachment of the associate teachers but, much more significantly, for the development of a mentoring culture within the school.

## The Selection of the Professional Mentor

In most cases in our study the professional mentor was recruited on a voluntary basis. In ten of the case study schools the post was occupied by a deputy head, in six it was a senior teacher, in three a head of department and in one an unpromoted teacher. The majority of the schools had been involved in a relatively long-term association with HEI and with the placement of students in teaching practice before the introduction of the partnership model of ITE. In these cases the member of staff who had been in place already was invariably invited to continue in role and, in many cases, was part of the development team charged with setting up the new structure. There was generally a very high level of motivation among professional mentors who were identified as the principal advocates for the involvement of their schools in ITE. Unlike the subject mentors, the professional mentor post had emerged, in every school, as a result of a consultative process, always with the involvement of the headteacher and usually the senior management team (SMT) as well. Whether or not the participation of the school in teacher education was considered to be central to the work of the school, the position of professional mentor was seen as an appointment of some importance and there was no shortage of senior staff to take it on.

The reasons given for staff to show such readiness to accept the extra responsibility varied from individual to individual. For some it had to do with investigating the possibility of a move into teaching in the HEI – 'I know I would like to move into that area of teaching' – or more generally to enhance career prospects. There was certainly seen to be career advantage in the development of the transferable administrative, organizational and managerial skills demanded for the role of professional mentor. Five of the professional mentors questioned felt that the work would provide evidence of management potential. For others it was to do with diversification at a time when they needed a career move: '...we attempt to ring the changes, for me this was to take on the professional development and ITE role which has given a whole new perspective and a different set of relationships'. For some professional mentors it was simply to do with enthusiasm for influencing the next generation of teachers. As one professional mentor put it, 'There is nothing in it financially...but I get a kick out of working with students and watching their development'.

## Payment and Time Allocation

The fact that the contractual relationship between school and HEI in ITE is so new meant that our case studies did not identify any common or generally established pattern of payment to professional mentors. In some cases there was no payment in terms of money. This was likely to be, for example, in situations where a deputy head in post had been working with the HEI for a number of years without payment and saw little in the new arrangements to merit additional remuneration. In other cases where the post had been advertised in the school and imposed additional responsibility, there was an honorarium or additional salary weighting. One headteacher explained that the funds were allocated to 'provide for an enhanced salary for the professional mentor so as to reflect the responsibility and status of the post'. In almost all the case study schools, however, the additional workload was acknowledged by the allocation of some, limited, time in which to shoulder the administrative burden. Typically, a professional mentor would receive 0.1 per cent of his or her timetable for the duties. Often it was only the professional mentor whose work was acknowledged as important in terms of additional payment and/or time and this undoubtedly caused resentment in schools where there was no corresponding payment for subject mentors. One subject mentor remarked with some feeling that 'the only person who gets most of the benefit is the so-called professional tutor, and as long as she gets her money and time, the rest don't matter at all'.

## Status and Influence

There is a very real sense in which the selection of the professional mentor reflected the way in which the school's involvement in ITE was perceived by the staff and particularly by the SMT of the school. In one of the case study schools the post of professional mentor was given as an additional responsibility to an unpromoted, main grade teacher who then found considerable difficulty in promoting the needs of the associate teachers, particularly with more senior members of staff. One such professional mentor acknowledged her inability to mediate on behalf of an associate with heads of department, 'who cannot be chased up in the way I would speak to one of my equals'.

In the majority of cases, however, the professional mentor held a position on the SMT. In ten schools it was as a deputy headteacher and in a further six as a senior teacher with other management responsibilities. The advantages of this model were widely acknowledged by staff interviewed in the schools, who saw it as essential for professional mentors to have 'access to every aspect of the school operation'. Typical of the views expressed is the comment from one mentor that, 'the fact that the professional mentor is also a senior teacher and an important member of the senior management team enables the views of the mentors and those of the university to be represented at a high level in the school in the meetings of the senior managers'.

Even where the professional mentor held a senior position in the school, there were widely differing perceptions of the role. In some schools it was seen to be, 'at an organizational rather than a conceptual level', involving a person who 'maintained the paperwork', and it seemed that 'the teacher education function was bolted onto the organization of the school'. The evidence presented for this assertion usually concerned the package of responsibilities associated with the post of professional mentor. In this bolt-on kind of organization the main responsibilities of the professional mentor had no obvious relevance to mentoring or the mentoring culture. In one school, for example, the professional mentor was also the examination secretary; in another the perceived main responsibility was as the senior teacher in charge of staff welfare who 'does not understand the college expectations of the enhanced role of the professional mentor as part of the training network'. She was perceived as seeing her role as 'facilitator and administrative backup...form filling and telephoning'.

At the other end of the spectrum there were examples of schools which were moving towards a model in which teacher education was perceived as an integral part of the school's work, where 'the SMT gave the changed scheme a high profile in the school'. In this model there was evidence of integration of teacher education into the development planning of the school. There was 'thinking within the school about the way in which we can provide opportunities for integration of student training and our own thinking about professional development'. Coherence was given to the professional mentor role by associating it with what were perceived to be complementary areas of responsibility such as appraisal and the induction of newly qualified teachers (NQT) or staff development. Schools did not all move or accept change at the same pace, but there was evidence in our study that the thinking was moving toward the 'integration' model even where it was not yet in place. One mentor remarked, 'The school has not yet integrated the professional development role, maintained by the other deputy, with the training role but the mentors are beginning to argue that it ought to be a possibility'.

## The Professional Mentor's Role

Within the HEI/school partnership model of ITE, the professional mentor has two main areas of responsibility:

- representing the interests of the school/HEI partnership
- the management of ITE in the school.

As stated above, we found that the professional mentor's interpretation of his/her role was influenced by the position held in the school and the extent to which ITE was or was not seen as an integral, important and permanent part of the work of the particular school. It was not surprising, therefore, that there should be variability between professional mentors both in their approach to their responsibilities and their capacity to carry them out.

## Representing the interests of the partnership

The professional mentor is or should be ideally placed to ensure that the nature of the partnership between school and HEI is understood and supported by both parties. In the partnership models we observed, the HEI management structure made provision for a professional mentor's committee with further representation on the partnership steering group or policy-making body. As a result of the meetings of these groups, effective communication between institutions was maintained and the interests of both school and HEI were served. It was seen as particularly important for the staff of the school to feel a sense of ownership of, and to be able to influence, the ITE process. It was suggested that this could best be delivered where the professional mentor had sufficient autonomy within the system to contribute to the effective operation of the various representative groups such as course planning and evaluation committees. This would ensure that the partnership operated effectively and would give the professional mentor the authority and status to establish and maintain the commitment of the school to the partnership. This is because he or she could represent and articulate the partnership thinking within the school from a position of involvement. It was not universally the case that the professional mentor considered that sufficient authority had been delegated for this to take place. In two of the case study schools all the decision making and representation of the school within the partnership were effectively the responsibility of the headteacher working through the professional mentor. But for the most part, the professional mentor was 'the key figure in the management'. A typical statement from one of the subject mentors was that 'the mentors identify with the professional mentor and recognize him as the contact between themselves and the SMT in the school and the university'.

Other facets of the professional mentor's role as representative of the partnership which were found in practice in our study schools, and which were perceived to strengthen the links between HEI and school, included the involvement of the professional mentor in the interviewing and selection of candidates for the ITE course, involvement in the course evaluation process, and the delivery of all or part of an education and professional studies course in the HEI. The professional relationship between the professional mentor and the link tutor in the HEI was seen as crucial in bringing coherence to the work of the school and the HEI, and a high proportion of those questioned believed that this relationship was effective in their experience.

## The management of ITE in the school

The management role of the professional mentor had a number of common features in all the case study schools, whatever the status of the post-holder. In every case it was expected that the professional mentor would negotiate with individual subject departments to have classes made available for associate teachers to teach, and to provide mentors with relevant experience and expertise to help and advise, supervise, monitor and assess them. The professional mentor was by definition the point of contact between the school and the HEI, with particular responsibility for liaison with the HEI link tutor and managing the attachment of the associates in the school. It was accepted in all cases that, in consultation with the HEI link tutor, the professional mentor would organize and contribute to the school-based course of study on whole school and cross-curricular issues and would take on the pastoral role for the associates during their school attachment. There were, however, marked variations between HEI partnerships and between schools within the same partnership in the way in which the professional mentor interpreted his/her role. Even where professional mentors were operating within the same HEI partnership and the key elements of management policy were stated in the partnership documentation, our research team found wide variations in management practice from school to school, much of which was determined by the nature of the school's perception of its level of involvement. Professional mentors accepted the contractual obligation to follow guidelines and ensure a degree of uniformity of practice but, as one of them said, it was 'with the understanding that we would use the mentoring handbook with a degree of flexibility'.

## Management of Associate Teachers

In the case study schools we found considerable differences in the magnitude of the management task in respect of the associates training in the school. The numbers of associates varied between two and 11 so that in a minority of schools, usually where the number of associate teachers was very small, there could be no real sense of group identity, the programme of school-based seminars did not take place as such, the individual associate had little or no contact with the professional mentor from day to day, and was introduced to the broader issues of the school largely on an ad hoc basis under the supervision of the subject mentor. In a much larger number of schools there was a well-established induction procedure for associate teachers and the provision of ample documentation to familiarize the associate teacher of the school's values, policies and practices in such matters as rewards and sanctions, pastoral responsibilities of form tutors, assessment procedures and the pattern of staff meetings and parents' evenings. There was, in all cases, a programme of seminars but not always evidence of the professional mentor interacting individually with the associates on a daily or even weekly basis. In a small number of schools at the other end of the spectrum, there was not only a well-established induction procedure and a programme of seminars to enable the associate to understand more completely the school's policies and practices, but the professional mentor had also organized formal meetings on a sometimes weekly, sometimes fortnightly basis with the group of associate teachers, for review and planning, and to reflect upon their experiences.

Observation of the associates in the classroom was another area where there was variation of practice from one professional mentor to another. In some schools the professional mentor did not consider it part of the role to observe lessons given by the associate teacher and this job was left to the subject mentor in collaboration with the curriculum tutor from the HEI. In other schools the professional tutor took it as part of his/her responsibility regularly to observe each associate teach and to prepare a written evaluation of the lesson or lessons, to provide an opportunity for debriefing, and to counsel the associate as needed.

## Management of Mentors

The professional mentors' management of the subject mentors began in most of our case study schools with the main responsibility for their appointment. For the most part this responsibility was shared with the headteacher or the relevant head of department, but we met some examples where the approach was made directly to staff members. One subject mentor said of two colleagues that 'they responded to personal invitation from the deputy head'.

The way in which the professional mentor viewed the relationship with the subject mentors varied from school to school. For professional mentors who had not yet fully appreciated the change from the traditional pattern of school practice and for whom the new model was of the bolt-on variety, the relationship had not moved beyond the administrative and organizational model. In this case the relationship effectively ended once the placement in the department and the provision of a subject mentor had been negotiated. Afterwards there was contact between professional and subject mentors only in reaction to some local difficulty or if the associate teacher was experiencing professional problems which required intervention from a third party. In one school it was expressed as follows: 'The relationship between professional tutor and mentors is a good one but not in the sense of being a team with a team leader. Meetings are called but not on a regular basis and appear to be either in response to Keele [HEI]-raised issues or to matters raised by the headteacher. It is a reactive not a proactive model'.

It was certainly the belief of those questioned that, in the first years of the HEI/school partnership, this model was the most common but that, increasingly, professional mentors were taking a view of themselves as leaders of a team of mentors within the school. Where this was the case, the professional mentor had ceased to be merely organizer and administrator and had assumed the role of facilitator, professional developer and quality controller of the teacher education process in the school. The management of the team of subject mentors involved the professional mentor in establishing the team, providing an induction programme, and developing, maintaining and supporting the team. The identification and selection of suitable mentors has already been mentioned above. The induction process was seen as a responsibility of the HEI in the first instance, but there was a perception in the case study schools that the professional mentor was the appropriate person to convene regular meetings of the mentor team which would serve to 'establish an atmosphere of openness in the school with those directly involved with the mentoring process', and at which they could discuss the important points of their training and their implications for the school.

This professional developmental role was seen by many of the mentors questioned as important. 'There is a strong feeling amongst the mentors that these meetings do take account of their views'. Another mentor comments that 'The way in which the professional mentor has developed a team approach has been appreciated and there is a feeling that we have gained from the cooperative activity'. Providing a forum in which mentors can compare notes, try out new ideas and share practice was widely welcomed. Such meetings had become the norm in at least half the schools studied and were held once or twice each term. They were considered useful not only for creating a sense of identity and mutual support among the mentors, but also as an avenue of communication with the SMT and the HEI. They presented 'a real opportunity to coordinate what we are doing, to communicate with the college through the professional mentor and to plan the activities...'.

## The School-based Programme of Study

The provision of a school-based programme of seminars on cross-curricular and whole school issues was a common feature of the role of the professional mentor in all the schools which participated in our research. In most cases the programme had evolved from a completely devolved model, in the early days of a partnership style of ITE, to a much more prescriptive programme which complemented the HEI course of education and professional studies. This sought to give associate teachers an insight into the policies and practices of the school and which complied with the partnership agreement, the Notes of Guidance of the Council for the Accreditation of Teacher Education (CATE) and the criteria as laid down by the DfE Circular 9/92.

As a result of this increased standardization there was less obvious variability of practice between schools and partnerships in this aspect of the professional mentors' work. Only in the very few examples mentioned above, where the numbers of associate teachers in the school was small, were the seminars either informal or non-existent. For most professional mentors there had been a process of negotiation, first with the link tutor from the HEI and then with staff in the school and, in some cases, with outside agencies to tap into the areas of expertise necessary for the delivery of the seminar programme.

In order to improve the quality of the school-based programme of study, the management role of the professional mentor had in a number of cases extended to liaison with other partnership schools to set up a joint programme of shared experiences in which groups of associate teachers might benefit from the seminar given by specialist staff from one or more other schools. Consortia of schools existing within the part-nership framework were also being used for other purposes such as the management of a second school experience, for example. In two groups of schools these consortia were 'beginning to look at whether we could do the whole job ourselves', rather than 'take time with the partnership arrangements which we are unable to control'.

## Monitoring and Assessment

Monitoring and assessment of the work of the associate teachers overall was an area in which there was some confusion. There have been misunderstandings reported concerning perceived professional mentor responsibility for the decisions to pass or fail a weak student, and there was a belief among some subject mentors that HEI curriculum tutors should take more responsibility, particularly in the assessment. In some cases professional mentors were apprehensive about the ability of the school staff to do the assessment without 'additional training and review of who does what'. In the partnership agreement with all the schools we studied there was, however, a clearly stated requirement that subject mentors had a responsibility for the assessment of practical and profes-sional teaching skills and that it was for the professional mentor to undertake a coordinating role in the monitoring and assessment of the associate teacher's work in the school.

We found that the professional mentor's capacity to fulfil this requirement depended to a considerable degree upon the nature of his/her relationship with the associate teachers. Where the role of the professional tutor was predominantly administrative and organizational and contact with the associate teachers was minimal once the induction process into the school was completed and the responsibility passed on to the mentors, the monitoring and assessment were, in effect, carried out by the subject mentors. In such cases there was perceived to be a danger of a lack of consistency of standards between departments, even within the same school. Where the professional mentor's role included at least a pastoral dimension and the associate teachers were offered support and encouraged to discuss tensions and difficulties with him/her, and where the work of the subject mentors was managed and moderated, then the professional mentor's ability to contribute to the monitoring and assessment process was proportionally greater. Where the professional mentor had developed an ITE team and fostered a professional relationship with mentors and with the associate teachers in the school, with formal meetings and opportunities to discuss their work and progress both with them and their mentors, there had emerged a climate in which the monitoring and assessment of the associates had become an integral part of the professional mentor's role.

## Models of Professional Mentor

It can be seen then that, at the particular time in the development of the HEI/school partnership model of ITE when the case studies were carried out, there was a wide diversity of interpretations of the professional mentor's role. All the schools in which case studies were carried out fell somewhere along the line between one in which mentoring was simply a bolt-on activity and one in which there was a mentoring culture embedded in and integral to the life of the school. Where head-teachers and school management teams perceived their involvement with the ITE partnership as temporary and, as one mentor put it, 'not seen as other than a goodwill offering on the part of the college', then the characteristics of the professional tutor role tended to reflect the attitude of the school.

At its least effective, the role was seen as bureaucratic in nature and the professional mentor's other responsibilities in the school were unrelated to it. There was no coherent policy for integrating ITE into the fabric of the school. The professional mentor dealt with individual subject mentors rather than a team and had little direct contact with the associate teachers in the school beyond the initial induction period and the provision of the school-based seminars. Meetings were infrequent and informal and the agenda driven by the HEI or the SMT or both. The mentors felt isolated, particularly where they had been given no real understanding of the contractual nature of the partnership model and they were frequently critical of the lack of support from the HEI tutors in curriculum areas. As one respondent suggested, 'none of the mentors see the role as either permanent or as a key to future development'.

In schools in which the involvement with the ITE partnership was seen to be an integral part of school life, where, as one professional mentor described the situation, 'the process hasn't changed the work of the school, it has become part of it', mentoring was seen as an area of major importance. In these circumstances it was likely that the school's involvement with teacher education was considered sufficiently important to be reported in the school development plan and that the appointment of the professional mentor was made only after considerable deliberation and in the light of other related responsibilities carried by senior staff. For one head teacher interviewed, the principal issue was 'that there needs to be an integrated approach to all staff development matters and mentoring is part of the total...the time has come to look at all aspects of staff development and not split-up jobs – there is a need to see that the mentoring process actually ties in with other aspects of staff development'. This view was typical of schools in which there was a strong mentoring culture where the professional mentor would be a senior colleague and expected to have a place on the SMT. Additional responsibilities might include the role of professional development coordinator or responsibility for NQTs or appraisal.

That the professional mentor should hold a senior post was considered vital by most of the subject mentors and associate teachers interviewed. It was felt necessary for the post-holder to carry weight with the tutors from the HEI and, more importantly, to ensure that the interests of ITE were adequately represented with senior colleagues in the work of the school. 'The fact that the professional tutor [mentor] was also a senior teacher and an important member of the senior management team, enabled the views of the mentors... to be represented at a high level in the school in the meetings of senior managers'. Ideally it was felt that the professional mentor should be a senior teacher rather than a deputy head because of the many responsibilities already carried by the latter. It was said by an associate of one professional mentor with other responsibilities as administrative deputy that, 'although she is very efficient, we don't feel she has time to give us all we need'.

In schools where our research identified a good mentoring climate, professional mentors' relationships with subject mentors and associate teachers had moved well beyond the 'administrative and organizational model' and were professional and developmental in character. Professional mentors and subject mentors were perceived as a team, and formal meetings between them, which were 'agendaed and minuted', were the norm. Similarly, the associate teachers felt that they were supported and assessed by a consistent and coordinated partnership of subject and professional mentors. It would not be true to say that any school included in our case study research exhibited all the characteristics of a 'mentoring culture', but the evidence suggests that best practice has taken account of the changes in the provision of ITE and has moved a long way toward a fully integrated and coordinated model.

# Reference

DfE 1992 *Initial Teacher Training (Secondary Phase)* Circular 9/92, London: DfE

*Chapter 6*

# Partnership

*Mervyn Taylor*

## The Framework for Partnership

The present arrangements for partnerships between secondary schools and HEIs were established under the framework of Circular 9/92 (DfE, 1992) which had as one of its three main principles that, 'schools should play a much larger part in ITT as full partners of higher education institutions (HEIs)' (para. 2).

The key phrase is 'full partners', for this represents the current view which can be seen as the latest elaboration of the idea of partnership, first expressed in 1984 in Teacher Training Circular 7/84. This began the long road towards the centralized control of teacher training provision which has characterized its development over the past 12 or 13 years. This centralizing tendency, meant to overcome the diverse autonomy which had characterized training previously and which was regarded as a contributor to the national failure of education to deliver appropriately trained and educated school-leavers, was supervised by a new body called CATE – the Council for the Accreditation of Teacher Education – whose role was to oversee, in a far more interventionist way, a national programme for initial teacher training. (Names do have a symbolic significance and it is interesting to note that the Council's name was defined in terms of 'education' rather than 'training'.) Under the new criteria designed to promote a more unified and systematic approach to training, it was required that all courses requiring accreditation should 'be developed and run in close working partnership with a number and variety of schools' (CATE, 1985, para. 3.2).

Little was said about the nature of these close working partnerships, and in any case, good training institutions were already involved in close working relations with their training schools. However, the requirements went further than this rather vague exhortation for it was also necessary that 'experienced teachers should be involved in the planning, supervision, support and assessment of students' practical work in schools, and in their training within the institution.' (CATE, 1985, para. 3.3).

For many engaged in training this was still the embodiment of good practice, but the last clause, suggesting that teachers should be involved in the institutional element in training, was more controversial, especially as little guidance was given as to how this might be actually achieved, given the nature of the demands on teachers in schools. However, the importance of this first set of criteria was not that they were just a set of guidelines for good practice, but rather that they were requirements to be fulfilled as a necessary pre-condition for the accreditation of courses and, therefore, recognition by the Secretary of State. Another requirement, seen at the time as much more of a threat to many trainers, was that those who were concerned with pedagogy should have had recent experience of teaching the age range for which they were preparing associates, that they should maintain regular and frequent experience of classroom teaching, and where this was not possible they should be given opportunities to demonstrate their teaching effectiveness in schools. The main reason for the inclusion of this was the government's claim that teacher trainers had become remote from the everyday demands of the classroom and that training in the basic skills of teaching – the craft of the classroom – had been downgraded at the altar of new, and often untried and untested, theories of learning, teaching and classroom organization.

In order to understand the development of partnerships, therefore, it is necessary to be aware of these two factors: first, that schools were to be more involved in teacher training so that it would have a more practical and down-to-earth approach and, second, there was an overwhelming distrust of the trainers, who were seen not only to be ineffective practitioners but also responsible for perpetuating an educational ideology which was at variance with the government's. It is an irony, therefore, that at the same time as the government were distrustful of teachers in schools and classrooms, and introduced their educational reforms to reduce teachers' autonomy and make them more accountable to local governors and parents, they also viewed them as being an essential and trustworthy element in the training of teachers, where it was the trainers who were regarded with suspicion.

This shift towards more school-based training was continued in the later part of the 1980s in a new circular which was issued in November

1989 (Circular 24/89) and this elaborated more fully on the idea of part-nership espoused five years earlier. Now it was proposed that HEIs should establish links, 'with local authorities and a number and variety of schools, and should develop and run the professional and educa-tional aspects of courses in close partnership with those schools' (Circular 24/89, para. 1.1). The important shift here is seen in the use of 'professional and educational aspects of courses' which extended the influence of practising teachers to cover most elements of training courses, but the nature of the partnership was still that of 'involvement'. Little was said concerning the role of LEAs but, in the elaboration of what partnership should actually mean for schools and HEIs, it was required that experienced teachers from the link schools should be involved in many aspects of course organization – planning and evalua-tion, selection of students, supervision and assessment of practical work, and should also make contributions to lectures and seminars on the HEIs' courses. So one can see the gradual extension of teacher involve-ment in the legal requirements of course accreditation; the guidelines, which CATE drew up to elaborate on these requirements, went even further as, for example, in the case of assessment, where instead of mere 'involvement' of teachers there was now to be a 'shared assess-ment' between schools and teacher trainers.

This further inclusion of teachers in the training of teachers posed few problems for the evolving training scene – again it emphasized good practice of the time – and viewed the development of partnership in an evolutionary way. On the other aspect of training, however, first detailed in the 1984 document, there was now included a much stronger requirement for trainers to get back into school for regular periods of refreshment and renewal of teaching experience; it seemed that, in order to achieve the goal of a more practical and relevant train-ing, Circular 24/89 demanded the re-training of the trainers – getting the trainers into school – rather than putting more of the training programme into schools.

In 1992, this latter policy was abandoned and a marked shift in direc-tion occurred. Gone was the emphasis on teacher trainers spending more time in school and in its place there was much greater significance attached to putting more of the training into the schools and giving teachers a much greater responsibility in that training: 'The planning and management of training courses should be the shared responsibility of higher education institutions and schools in partnership' (Circular 9/92, para. 1.2). This would appear to mark the arrival of equality in training between schools and HEIs and indeed the language of the Circular now signifies 'responsibilities' rather than 'involvement' and envisages schools as having joint responsibility for most aspects of training courses. However, Circular 9/92 went further than this and, in the preamble to the accreditation criteria, there was set out what the government 'expected' to be the balance of responsibilities, in specific areas of course programmes, as between schools and HEIs: 'Schools will have a leading responsibility for training students to teach their specialist subjects, to assess pupils and manage classes; and for supervising students and assessing their competences in these respects' (Circular 9/92, para. 14).

This placed far more responsibility and work onto schools. The expectation of government went much further than the accreditation criteria for courses which more frequently referred to 'institutions and their partner schools' in the spirit of a joint responsibility for the various aspects of training. From the above quotation it can be seen that it is now the schools who are expected to have the leading responsibility for the central aspects of training. HEIs, on the other hand, are given the lead responsibility for academic validation, presenting courses for accreditation, awarding qualifications and arranging placements. Not even quality control is mentioned as a legitimate lead responsibility for HEIs, even though certification is achieved through a higher education institution. So, on the one hand is the rhetoric of joint responsibility, juxtaposed with a different view on the other – that most aspects of training should be the lead responsibility of schools. It is as though teacher training institutions were to franchise out most of their operations to schools, as indeed has happened in those cases where schools themselves can take on sole responsibility for training.

This expectation of government raises questions of both a philosophical and practical concern. In the first place, what does 'lead responsibility' actually mean? Does it mean that schools will be chiefly responsible for the planning and delivery of course programmes? If so, how can this actually be achieved in a partnership which may involve up to 50 different schools and over 200 teachers? Do teachers, primarily responsible for teaching children, want this degree of responsibility and if so, how can they find the time to be able to do this? Whether schools are fulfilling these 'expectations' of government, or indeed whether they wish to do so, may become clearer as the nature of how partnerships are developing is explored in this chapter.

## The Development of Partnership

Whether partnerships develop according to the accreditation criteria only, that is according to a more equally shared set of responsibilities between schools and HEI, or whether they develop according to the government's expected criteria, with schools taking the lead in most aspects of training, there are still a number of organizational problems which have to be addressed. The first of these concerns the take-up of the new role of mentor for those teachers in schools who take on the responsibility of looking after trainee teachers as part of their job. This role of mentor within the shared partnership arrangement is a new one; it is not the principal duty of the teacher, for that is teaching children. This new role is an additional one and, as Wilkin (1992) suggests, one that goes very much further than that of the teacher looking after an associate while on traditional teaching practice. All these new roles of mentor and professional tutor require new skills and additional time – for a properly structured programme of induction into the school and the subject department; to assist the new teachers in their planning of lessons; to observe lessons or parts of lessons so that they can be appropriately debriefed – these are but three of many additional duties now required of mentors, as reviewed in earlier chapters. What has happened to teacher training, therefore, as a result of partnership development, is not that a large part of the HEI element of training has been handed over to schools because, in fact, there is little additional time required in schools compared with previous PGCE courses; rather it is the case that what previously passed for training in schools was usually unsystematic and ad hoc, with little being asked for by the HEI, and what was given by way of support from the school was usually on a grace and favour basis, often because of the interest and enthusiasm of individual teachers. There was no feeling at all that there was, or should be, a whole school involvement with, and responsibility for, training; associates merely came into school to practice on 'our' children and while, of course, there was a professional approach to dealing with associates, they were very often regarded as a somewhat inconvenient necessity – a kind of duty to the profession which some teachers felt obliged to undertake.

Now, however, the task in school has to be approached in a more systematic and unified way; training procedures have to be well organized and well planned, with appropriate time given to mentors to fulfil this function appropriately. The roles and duties of mentors have had to be defined more precisely and so with partnership the whole concept and organization of training within the schools has become far more systematic and professional. If, in the past, teachers felt less than enthusiastic about the nature and quality of some of the training, then equally the HEI felt unable to burden the school with requests for the additional input necessary for a more systematic training programme for the new teachers within the school. With partnership, all this has changed dramatically and teachers now feel a sense of ownership of the training process, a view supported by Everton and White (1992). A number of mentors recorded in their interviews that the greatest motivating factor for being part of the training process was the input 'into the training of their own profession', encouraging others to be good teachers and seeing the improvement in the associate teacher, in terms of confidence and skill, over the year. Despite all the difficulties of developing partnership, therefore, this degree of commitment from mentors is impressive and represents a definite improvement on what usually occurred before.

Again, there is an irony, for the move to partnership was, in part, ideologically-driven, an attempt by government to control the trainers by giving more responsibility to schools, even though training in the schools was pretty variable. What is actually happening, however, is that through a sharing of the training between schools and HEI, with each side beginning to identify and clarify the nature of the contribution which each can make towards training, a better system of training is now the result, as shown by HMI reports.

## Mentors' Perceptions of Partnership

The mentors' views on the nature of partnership are important indicators of how the new structures of training are being received in schools. Certainly, as with most in HEIs, the idea of partnership itself is regarded as a welcome development, with 92 per cent of mentors agreeing that they are a move in the right direction. Also, as shown in Table 6.1, the HEI contribution to partnership is valued, with 92 per cent of mentors affirming its contribution as important or very important, with only 8 per cent regarding it as not very important. Of considerable significance is the mentors' answer to the question, who should pass or fail the associate teachers' practical teaching? This is not only an area of practical organization, it is also the symbolic entry point of new teachers into the profession and it is a decision of immense importance which needs to be made with fairness and good judgement. Over three-quarters of mentors felt that this should be a partnership decision, with only 20 per cent suggesting that it should be the school's decision alone. This would seem to suggest that mentors do want the support of the HEI and that, at present, they do not want to take on the 'leading responsibility' as outlined in Circular 9/92, even for the assessment of practical teaching; what they wish to be is equal partners in the enterprise.

**Table 6.1** *Mentors' opinions on partnership (%)*

|  | *Yes* | *Not sure* | *No* |
|---|---|---|---|
| Is partnership a move in the right direction? | 92.1 | 6.9 | 1.0 |
|  | *Very important* | *Important* | *Not V. Imp.* |
| The importance of HEI to training | 51.0 | 41.0 | 8.0 |
|  | *School* | *HEI* | *Partnership* |
| Responsibility for pass/fail in teaching | 20.0 | 4.0 | 76.0 |

How the partnership may develop in the future is another issue, but again, in answer to the question concerning the most benefit to associate teachers in the future, 63 per cent of mentors felt that the present pattern should continue, with less than one-third suggesting greater school control than at present (see Table 6.2). The predominant view was summed up by one mentor who suggested that, 'the school was, and still is, an institution for educating pupils and not for training prospective teachers. We don't want the balance of input into initial teacher education to be too heavily weighted on the school as the education of our pupils is our first priority'.

However enthusiastic schools might be for the new pattern of training, to set up a new structure and organization for training takes a considerable amount of time (though Circular 9/92 allowed a very short time-scale for the introduction of the new procedures). The Keele partnership began earlier than most, in 1991, based on the Oxford Internship model, but even so, the establishment of new roles for mentors naturally causes some anxiety and concern, even if many

**Table 6.2** *Mentors' views concerning the most benefit to future generations of trainee teachers (%)*

|  | Continue present pattern | Greater HEI control | Greater school control | Other arrangement |
|---|---|---|---|---|
| Of most benefit to future trainee teachers | 62.9 | 4.1 | 27.8 | 5.2 |

teachers welcome the opportunity to become more involved in training. One of the main challenges in the organization and management of partnerships is that of ensuring good communication between the schools and the HEI. Different partnerships have different models of organization, so it is not always possible to generalize; however, it would be fair to claim that it is easier to maintain communication between each school's professional mentors and the HEI, than it is to maintain close communication between individual mentors and other mentors and the HEI. The problem is one of logistics and geography. For example, if there are a relatively large number of students within each school, say between six and eight – and the trend is for larger groups within schools so that appropriate support programmes can be provided – then 35 schools will cater for about 250 students. Keeping contact with that group as a whole and with the professional mentor is not too difficult, given that one HEI tutor is responsible for liaising with two schools. However, with the case of mentors the situation is different, for there may be four or five mentors in each school and these teachers cover different subject areas. If liaison is to be maintained between mentors and the curriculum subject tutor within the HEI then this becomes a much more difficult problem, for the curriculum tutor has to be involved with many schools – maybe 15 or more – which creates difficulties in providing the continuity of contact and the degree of support which mentors appear to want. In the Keele partnership, out of the 97 mentors responding, 69 (68 per cent) felt that communication between the HEI and school was well managed, with 12 per cent disagreeing; it is worth noting the rather large percentage of all responses which were placed within the 'not sure' category in Table 6.3, perhaps a reflection of mentors' inexperience or their lack of criteria with which to judge the efficacy of these new training arrangements.

**Table 6.3** *Mentors' views on communication and support of HEI tutors within the partnership (%)*

|  | Agree | Not sure | Disagree |
|---|---|---|---|
| Communication between school and HEI well managed | 68.1 | 19.8 | 11.9 |
| HEI tutors supportive of mentors' work | 82.3 | 12.5 | 5.2 |
| HEI tutors and mentors share the same values | 62.0 | 30.0 | 8.0 |
| HEI has provided adequate training for mentors | 49.0 | 31.0 | 20.0 |
| HEI tutors supportive with weaker trainee teachers | 58.7 | 34.8 | 6.5 |

Most mentors agreed that the HEI tutors were generally supportive of mentors' work and a majority (62 per cent) felt that they had shared values with the HEI tutors, though again over one-third are unsure or disagree. One thing is quite clear from Table 6.3, however: there is a need for more mentor training, as only about half of them felt that they had been adequately trained. This represents another challenge within partnerships, for as subject requirements change and mentors move between schools, there is a need for continuous training and professional development programmes. As for HEI tutors being supportive of weaker trainee teachers, the high response in the 'not sure' category may be due to the fact that a number of mentors had little or no experience within their own subject area of a weaker associate and, therefore, were not sure whether the HEI gave appropriate support; certainly the percentage who disagree is very small.

## Associate Teachers' Perceptions of Partnership

One can see from the data presented in the previous section that mentors generally welcome the idea of partnership and the new arrangements for training. What of the associate teachers; how do they see these developments? Of course, from the associate teachers' viewpoint, many of the structural features of partnership organization will not be apparent; rather, it is the day-to-day interactions which are most visible and, like the concert pianist who plays a wrong note, it is when things go wrong that communication and coordination appear to be lacking. This may occur if there is insufficient support from the HEI, or inappropriate mentoring in the school, or when there are different expectations or different ideologies coming from different sides of the partnership and, of course, disagreements between tutors. These are the areas of partnership which are most salient to associate teachers.

Table 6.4 shows the associate teachers' perceptions of communication between the HEI and the school, and it reveals that two out of three feel that it is well managed, with the remainder recording that it is not. This is about the same proportion as for mentors and while it shows that there has been considerable progress in the structure and organization of partnership, it also demonstrates that there are difficulties in achieving consistent patterns of information and expectations across a large number of different schools and mentors.

**Table 6.4** *Associate teachers' perceptions of the partnership (%)*

|  | Yes | No |
|---|---|---|
| Communication between HEI/school well managed | 66.5 | 33.5 |
| Tutors and mentors coordinate work | 66.5 | 33.5 |
| Educational values shared by HEI and school | 61.4 | 38.6 |

This can be particularly the case with different subject areas, as there may be different emphasis and different requirements between subjects at particular points in the training programme. About two-thirds of associate teachers also felt that there was good coordination between the mentors and HEI tutors, but there is still the problem that a relatively large proportion feel that there is here a discontinuity. There are always bound to be different emphases on the values of the HEI and the school, for they are different institutions serving different needs. This can work both ways, for one associate teacher claimed, 'I feel that the idealism and ethos of good educational practice engendered, encouraged and actively promoted by the HEI was sadly lacking in the schools. Innovation and imagination were encouraged in the HEI and frowned upon in school', while another suggested that 'part of the training in the HEI seemed to be far removed from the real world and not geared towards the realities of teaching'.

This balance between theory and practice, between different kinds of ethos and the different contributions which each side of the partnership makes to the whole, is part of the tension which is bound to exist within partnerships and which is also subject to individual associate teachers' expectations of what they want and need from a PGCE course; such tension should not be regarded as unwelcome but should rather be seen in a creative way, the grit in the oyster, which moves good practice forward for both kinds of institutions.

In evaluating the contribution of school and HEI to the training programme, it is natural to expect that the school is viewed as very important – one simply couldn't train as a teacher without school experience – but perhaps the most interesting feature is the way the associate teachers perceive the HEI contribution to training, with 78 per cent claiming it is important or very important, again emphasizing the success of partnership as a joint enterprise in the training of teachers.

**Table 6.5** *Associate teachers' views on the importance for training of schools and HEI*

|  | Very important | Important | Not really important | Not important at all |
|---|---|---|---|---|
| How important is the HEI contribution | 26.0 | 52.5 | 16.4 | 5.1 |
| How important is the school contribution | 79.3 | 14.5 | 5.0 | 1.1 |

While the idea of partnership as a model for training is welcomed, there are still perceived problem areas which need to be addressed. One of these is that different criteria may be used by schools and HEI in judging the progress of associate teachers and assessing their teaching skills at particular points in the course. This is always a difficult area, and associate teachers report that common criteria are used between mentors and tutors mostly or always in 62 per cent of cases; but 30 per cent claim that common criteria are used only sometimes, and 7 per cent suggest that this is a rarity. Good communication, frequent mentor meetings and a more comprehensive sharing of expectations might assist in this regard, though the gradual development of teaching skills is not an orderly set of emerging competences, but rather a discontinuous and uneven process which proceeds at different rates and different times. Taken as a whole, however, the associate teachers appear to like these new partnership based courses for, when asked if the course had lived up to expectations, 56 per cent rated it as better than expected, with 34 per cent suggesting it was as expected and less than 10 per cent recording that it had not lived up to expectations.

No matter how good structures are, in the final analysis much depends on the people who have to carry out their roles and responsibilities and on the quality of relationships which they develop with each other and with the trainee teachers. As one associate teacher reported, 'The course was good for me. My mentor at school was first rate and I feel confident about taking up my post in September. The HEI backed up the practice very well. I'm glad that it has not been easy sailing as my experience will undoubtedly help me in my teaching career'.

## Funding Partnership

The funding arrangements for partnerships remain one of the chief areas of concern for all those engaged within teacher training. Two main areas affect policy development: first, the amount of funding which is devolved from the HEI to partner schools and for what purpose and, second, how that funding is distributed and used within individual schools in the partnership. On both counts it is difficult to obtain reliable and meaningful information from both schools and HEI.

### Global funding

Looking solely at the actual amount of funding transferred from HEI to schools is not a very meaningful exercise, because what also has to be ascertained is the kind of provision which is being made by the school for that amount of funding. The situation becomes additionally complex because of the different partnership arrangements which may exist between institutions and schools; for example, partnerships which have two blocks of school experience of nearly equal length may fund first and second school experiences differently to reflect the different degree of input required by the first and second school. Some partnerships provide funding for a brief primary experience; other partnership arrangements, which are closer to the Oxford model and which require associates to spend the majority of the time with one school, facilitate a less complicated financial arrangement as one school is responsible for nearly all the school-based tasks. Other HEIs arrange for a proportion of funding to be made on the basis of INSET provision, thus making it difficult to provide an overall costing of the training package. All this variation makes it extremely difficult to provide meaningful compar-isons between different partnerships and to estimate a national norm as to what HEIs are devolving to schools for each trainee per year. Furthermore, the amount of funding devolved has been changing rapidly over the last two or three years as partnerships have gradually developed to meet the September 1994 deadline, laid down in Circular 9/92, for the new training arrangements to be in place. An example may show the typical escalation of funding; in the Keele University Partnership in 1992–3, the funding devolved to schools was £350 per associate teacher, in 1993–4 it was £650 and in 1994–5 it is £1,050. The sum of around £1,000, either in cash or kind, seems to be the modal figure, but there are considerable deviations from that; this seems now quite close to the Secondary Heads Association's (SHA) analysis which proposed a figure of £1,400 per year for what the schools provide. However, great caution is required to interpret all these estimates as the range of services which they 'buy' from schools varies enormously, such as in training new mentors and in the actual cost of running and main-taining the partnership as an organization.

The transfer of such large sums can begin to change the nature of the relationship between HEI and schools and also between departments within HEIs themselves. First, HEIs have to set up new accounting, transfer and monitoring systems to actually transfer such large amounts of money, often in excess of £250,000. Second, the criteria and methods of funding education departments within universities has also become more visible and what has frequently come to light is that, in the past, education departments have been a very profitable sector within HEIs, generating large sums of money for research and development else-where within institutions. Whether the new Teacher Training Agency will allow funds earmarked for teacher training to be used within other faculties within HEIs is yet to be decided, but this will be a critical area of decision making. The other factor which has placed great pressure within education departments is that the unit of funding has declined since the average figure of £3,750 for each secondary PGCE associate was announced in Circular 9/92. It is now difficult to give an overall figure as the average unit of funding varies so much between institu-tions; this is partly a result of so-called efficiency savings as well as a change in the method for distributing additional associates, with HEIs being encouraged to bid for additional students at lower costs. The effects of this have meant that education departments are continuing to

receive extra money in addition to getting extra hands'. This raises the whole question of the benefits which accrue to the school from having a sizeable group of new, though inexperienced, teachers in the school. As one head of a partner school attested, 'From the school's point of view, effective mentoring can be stimulating, satisfying and professionally developmental for colleagues, offering hitherto unobtainable facets of professional experience to committed and successful classroom teachers. At the same time the youth, vigour and enthusiasm of associates often brings a welcome breath of fresh air into many schools faced with the inexorable rise in the age of staff'. There is clearly a need for a detailed cost/benefit analysis of the involvement in partnerships by schools, undertaken by an independent body such as the Audit Commission, in order that better financial management and provision may be mapped out in the future.

The whole question of the distribution of funding within schools raises serious problems, for if the school adopts a whole school approach to training, which it should, then every teacher is to some extent involved and payment to selected individuals only may be seen as divisive. On the other hand, if mentors are made responsible for organizing and delivering appropriate mentoring support, then there is a strong case for giving recognition in terms of remuneration and status for such a task, as is the case for general professional development within schools. Perhaps as partnership arrangements stabilize, this is something on which there may emerge a national consensus orchestrated by the teachers' professional associations.

## Conclusion

Partnerships are at an early stage in their evolution and it will take a few more years before a proper evaluation of their impact on training can be made. Much will depend on the attitude of government and whether it feels that partnerships go far enough in satisfying their basic ideological needs as well as providing good quality training. As far as the latter is concerned, the signs are promising for, as has been argued earlier, it is primarily due to the school side of training being transformed, with increased commitment, better organization and more carefully thought-out provision and support. Both mentors and associates appear to welcome the new partnership arrangements even if, naturally, there are difficult organizational and communication problems which will always need addressing. The schools do not appear to want to take the lead responsibility for the majority of the training programmes but rather appear to want a partnership of equals within the training process.

Partnerships present many new opportunities for exploring curriculum development, in-service training and research, as well as providing good quality teacher training. In one of the partnerships investigated, summer term activities for associates included the evolution, preparation and trialling of materials for GNVQ courses, the use of team teaching for problem solving and investigation work in mathematics, and an intensive support system for pupils with special learning needs. The potential is there for increased opportunities for genuinely collaborative research and evaluation, something which mentors themselves believe is important for partnership development and a move which may be encouraged by the promise of more stability within the National Curriculum. The one area of real concern remains the financial basis of partnership because the present arrangements threaten the financial viability of education departments within HEIs. If the expertise for subject development and research into teaching and learning which exists in departments is eventually lost, then the future in schools may see a National Curriculum which becomes rather stale, repetitive and ossified, and which fails to provide that element of creativity and innovation which should characterize any national system of education and training.

# References

Council for the Accreditation of Teacher Education 1985 *Criteria for Approval of Teacher Education Courses,* London: DfE.

DfE 1984 *Teacher Training (Secondary Phase),* Circular 7/84, London: DfE.

DfE 1989 *Criteria for Initial Teacher Training Course Accreditation,* Circular 24/89, London: DfE.

DfE 1992 *Initial Teacher Training (Secondary Phase),* Circular 9/92, London: DfE.

Everton, T and White, S (1992) 'Partnership in training: the University of Leicester's new model of school based teacher education', *Cambridge Journal of Education,* 22, 2.

Wilkin, M (1992) 'On the cusp: from supervision to mentoring in initial teacher training', *Cambridge Journal of Education,* 22, 1.

*Chapter 7*

# The Departmental Perspective

*Tricia Evans*

While much has been written in recent years concerning the general impact of initial teacher training partnership schemes upon the school, less has been written in relation to the effect of such schemes upon specific curriculum areas. Much attention has been paid to the general skills and qualities required of mentors, less to the demands made of mentors in a particular subject department.

Different subject departments may share essential teaching methodologies but their stated aims and views of their own distinctive contributions to the whole school curriculum will diverge. Secondary school teachers will affiliate themselves with and usually feel an allegiance to the department team, before any other in the school. In many cases a sense of strong department identity and shared assumptions will develop, which may be recognized in the perceptions of other staff: 'You'll have to win over the scientists...', 'The English department won't want to relinquish mixed ability teaching in the lower school'. A subject department's shared values may be reflected in those of a group of single subject mentors, such that HEI curriculum tutors will not only be aware of the implicit and explicit values and assumptions of the groups of mentors with which they meet and work but will also, informally, be aware of how these differ from those of other mentor groups. While an administrative consistency is ultimately applied to schools by partnership management processes, experience suggests that a more fundamental, and intangible, diversity of approach and belief, in large part bedded in subject differences, flourishes beneath this surface.

The experience of working with English mentors for three years within a developed partnership scheme, and with English supervisors within schools for ten years prior to this, has indicated that among those mentoring English PGCE students a significant consensus exists. This relates to the qualities and skills demanded of the English mentor, the benefits and problems associated with mentoring, and to the particular nature of English mentors and their associates. It also appears that mentors have followed a variety of routes into the role. While they have not taken this on for financial reward, having become aware of the workload involved, some are beginning to press for appropriate compensation, particularly through safeguarded mentoring time. Discussions with English mentors have indicated that they welcome associate teachers and will continue to do so, but that all have had difficulties in fulfilling the role as they would wish through a lack of time. The outcomes of mentor meetings and informal discussions with individual mentors have suggested that a key factor in the mentor's attitude to mentoring in general is the calibre of the last associate teacher they received, typified by comments such as, 'You always send us such good students but I don't think we'd have the capacity for a poor one'; 'I suddenly realized how much time I'd given to supporting the associate. I thought twice before agreeing to another one'.

Such an apparent consensus can of course be illusory: the result of meetings involving mentors from the same partnership, which are managed in such a way that consensus is encouraged and reinforced while divergent views are suppressed through inertia, apprehension, or an unwillingness to rock the boat. Curriculum tutors chairing such meetings have considerable scope for promoting not just the mentoring demands of the partnership, generally promulgated through a steering committee and the professional mentors (who tend to constitute a more cohesive and powerful group than the many and disparate mentors), but also for reinforcing their own views of the role of the mentor. Some mentors may find it easier to toe the line of acceptance of HEIs and curriculum tutors' definition of their role rather than dispute and reform this, particularly given that mentoring is inevitably not at the heart of their school job profile.

This chapter records the outcomes of a research study which was undertaken in order to examine the views of English mentors across a range of partnership schemes; in order to identify consensus and disparity of view concerning the rewards, benefits and problems associated with mentoring English associate teachers; and to gain greater insight into how schools and HEIs could help to support English mentors in their role. The survey discloses mentors' personal views of their confidence, or lack of it, to discharge their role, their sense of lack of empowerment to influence the ways in which English associates are trained, and their assessment of the validity of the partnership.

## The Nature of the Sample

Twelve mentors, responsible between them for 23 PGCE English students during the school year in which the study took place, were interviewed in 12 different schools. Eleven to 16 and 11 to 18, secular and denominational, inner-city, suburban and semi-rural schools were all included in the sample, drawn from a representative range of catchment areas, from the most to the least advantageous. The numbers on roll ranged from 600 to 1,700. The schools were in partnership with seven higher education institutions: five universities and two institutes of higher education. The partnerships ranged from those which had been developed over a number of years to those which were relatively new.

The English departments from which the mentors were drawn varied in size from one with 12 full-time members of staff to one with only four. Departments accepted between one and three English associate teachers but the majority received two at any one time. The English mentors fulfilled a range of other roles within the school: one was also a senior teacher, two headed the English department, one was a head of year, one was in charge of the library, five were second in the department (including two who were acting head of the department), and only two were department members without other specified responsibilities.

Mentors' experience of teaching English in maintained secondary schools ranged from one who had taught English for 24 years to one who had only five years' experience. Three had been teaching English in secondary schools for five to ten years, seven for ten to 20 years and two for more than 20 years. The mean number of years in secondary English teaching was 14. While one mentor (now a senior teacher) had been supervising students in pre- and post-partnership programmes over a period of 19 years, and one mentor had begun only the previous year, the average number of years experience of supervising students was five. The interval between commencing secondary school English teaching and supervising students ranged from two to 18 years (the former being a young teacher in the smallest school in the sample). The average interval was nine years. Not surprisingly, most mentors were participating in relatively young partnership schemes; 50 per cent of those interviewed had first become 'mentors' in the previous year and the remaining half had fulfilled the role for between two and four years.

Of the nine who had switched from being supervisors in pre-partnership schemes to being mentors, only one could identify any corresponding change of role or status, and this was described as only being a 'gradual shift of emphasis'.

All the associate teachers the mentors had worked with in partnership schemes had been following one-year PGCE courses and were specializing in the teaching of English. The structure of the courses varied between those involving a substantial secondary teaching practice in one school, with a minor teaching experience in a second secondary school, those incorporating two secondary teaching experiences in the same school, and one HEI requiring three different secondary teaching experiences. All the courses incorporated a preliminary familiarization period in which associate teachers spent a short period of time, typically one or two days a week, in either their minor or main school. The English mentors were not critical of the essential structure of the PGCE course; indeed, almost all seemed to accept the fact that the course framework had been devised by HEI tutors and that the structure was not open to meaningful question by mentors. Not one had played a significant part in overall course design; where school staff had been involved, professional mentors had been consulted, rather than mentors. No English mentor had played a part in selecting associate teachers, either for the course or for their school. Of the two mentors who had been offered the option of jointly interviewing applicants with the HEI curriculum tutor, one was defeated by inescapable teaching commitments, and the other preferred to accept the associates selected by the university department. Of the remainder, who were not offered this option, six would have liked to have participated in the selection procedures for the course, rather than for the school.

## The Route into Mentoring

Of those interviewed, three mentors were invited to take on the role by the professional mentor, three volunteered and two saw it as a natural consequence of being head of department. One was 'flattered into it' by the professional mentor; one was invited by the head of department and subsequently persuaded by the professional mentor; one was persuaded by the headteacher; and one 'slid into the role as a consequence of being a member of a working party convened by the HEI'.

When the seven mentors who had been invited to take on the role were asked to state what they conjectured to be the reason for their selection, four focused upon the perceived quality of their teaching: 'The professional mentor has a high opinion of my teaching. He knows I'm enthusiastic about classroom teaching and it's this aspect of the job which is most relevant for students in training'. 'I was told I'd been chosen because of the excellent standards of my classroom management, because of my youth and I was also thought to have more time available because I'm not a head of department'. One mentor cited her personal qualities as likely reasons for her selection: 'I feel I was chosen because of my interpersonal skills. I'm welcoming and approachable'. Another mentor viewed her selection less positively: 'They were looking for someone without significant management responsibilities'. Those mentors selected were, without exception, chosen by the school, and the professional mentor played an influential part in this selection, either covertly through approaching the headteacher or a deputy head, or through a direct approach to the potential mentor. In all cases of selection of mentors the criteria for this were not formally documented, and where an indication of the criteria was given (in three of the seven cases), this was only formally orally stated in one case. Elsewhere the criteria remained implicit: 'The professional mentor came to me and said, "You'd make a good mentor"'; 'I knew implicitly what he was looking for because of my earlier relationship with him'.

Two of those who volunteered for the role were also head of department. This fact seemed to induce a sense of obligation to protect other department members: 'I felt I should take the responsibility, particularly since it was a new initiative'; 'I didn't want an already pressurized department to be over-burdened'. This was inverted, interestingly, by a mentor who was a long-serving second in the department and who felt that it was unfair to add to the head of department's responsibilities by expecting him to act as mentor too. One mentor had volunteered as a second in the department as part of the departmental role distribution, before it was decided by the senior management team that all those who were second in their departments should become mentors. One young mentor had volunteered because he enjoyed working with students, having only recently qualified himself. He had seen himself as fitting the role, particularly when compared with more obvious contenders: 'The head of department is not really in touch with the experience of new teachers, and experienced members of staff plough their own furrow. I feel I am more open to new ideas and ways of working'. Another, again significantly young, mentor explained that she had volunteered because, 'The school has quite a large number of older staff. I saw mentoring as a way of getting fresh, new staff into the department'. This was echoed by another mentor: 'We're a very middle-aged male department. I felt it would be good to have young – and female – students in'.

Mentors typically cited the potentially beneficial impact of trainees on their own professional development and job satisfaction when stating why they had taken on the role of mentor: 'It's an enjoyable part of our work and there's so much to learn as a mentor'. 'I thought it would be exciting – and it has been – and a good career move'. Several mentors emphasized the challenge involved in training the English teachers of the future: 'I wanted to become a mentor because if we don't contribute, invest, then we can't expect the pay back and we can't argue with the quality of teachers if we haven't played our part'. 'I saw it as a challenge. There's a tendency, if we're not careful, to reject students because they're a risk. I want to give students a chance as I was'.

Three-quarters of the mentors felt that the rest of the department had supported their adoption of the role. However, of these, three reported that the support was qualified by ignorance, resentment or relief: 'They were supportive but there was perhaps a lack of knowledge of the time commitment required. Originally other members of the department seemed to see the mentor's job as a bit of a perk'. 'They supported me but there was some resentment because of the extra work they thought it would entail for others'. 'Other members of the department were glad they didn't have to do it, even though they had more experience as student supervisors'. One mentor was unsure of the response of other department members and one reported indifference which, ironically, seemed to be rooted in similar sentiments to those quoted above: 'Given the demanding nature of the job, they were more or less indifferent'. One mentor noted the problem caused by applications from three department members for the role of mentor, which was only resolved by accepting one student for each applicant.

When asked to describe their induction into mentoring from the time of their acceptance of the role to their first meeting with associate teachers, mentors, without exception, alluded to the training provided centrally by the HEI. A variety of patterns for training provision were cited: one three-hour session, half a day, one and a half days, two days, 'twilight' sessions and cluster meetings. Half the mentors described a schedule which commenced with training based at the HEI which was generally followed, soon after, by a training meeting within the school, involving the professional mentor and other mentors. The remainder of those questioned described induction as commencing with a training meeting organized by the professional mentor for all mentors within the school, as a prelude to the training sessions provided by the HEI. There was a general acceptance by the mentors that some form of initial training, provided by the HEI, was necessary. However, one mentor described this as, 'useful in its way but not a good preparation for being a mentor', and another described its value only in terms of providing opportunities to talk with other mentors, particularly with those more experienced in the role. It was apparent that the training provided less formally within schools, exclusively through meetings involving the school's mentors and professional mentor, was held in higher regard and had made more impact upon mentors that the training provided by the HEIs.

Mentors' description of the training provided after the induction initiatives indicated a patchy and fragmented situation. Four mentors stated that they had received no training of any kind since; one suggested that any 'training' had come incidentally through the occasional visits of the curriculum tutor; three indicated that any further training had come through meetings with the professional mentor. The remainder typically described two or three refresher meetings. One mentor outlined a formal pattern of termly English mentor meetings which she had found helpful in providing a forum for the exchange of ideas. Two of those mentors who had received no further training anticipated that mentor meetings of this kind would prove helpful. When asked to assess the quality of the training they had received, mentors were generally critical of that provided by the HEI and appreciative of that provided within the school: 'The training offered by the university was rather thin, particularly for those who had never supervised students before. We need to discuss the issues with teachers who have done the job before'. 'The training did not suggest a real partnership. It merely spelt out what was required but there was no opportunity for mentors to make an impact'. 'The training provided by the college was of limited value. The most valuable training and support came from the department – particularly from those who'd done the job before – and from the professional mentor'.

However, one mentor described the training provided by the HEI as being of a high standard; another felt that the two days of initial training had been 'very informative, but I don't think I'd gain anything from further sessions of this type. Further support and training is best provided by the professional mentor'. All the mentors felt that further ongoing training and support of some kind would be beneficial. However, there was a general feeling that little more training would be provided by the HEI and that mentors would do well to look to the professional mentor for support in the future. Several mentors anticipated that HEIs would no longer be able to fund mentor training. This might have a considerable impact on subject-based work.

## Mentors' Understanding of their Role

The English mentors stressed the multiplicity and complexity of their roles. They saw themselves pre-eminently as supporters, counsellors and facilitators. Several framed their responses in terms of the practical and personal: 'It's about providing guidance and security, ensuring that both the student and the class are happy. It's the mentor's role to ensure that students understand the practicalities and that their personal needs are catered for'. 'My role is one of supporting, listening, discussing and opening out issues in a practical way rather than a theoretical way...for example, dealing with the disruptive pupil'.

While half of the mentors referred in passing to their role in liaising with the HEI, the remainder made no mention of the HEI at all at this point and seemed to imply a distinctive role for the mentor which almost excluded the HEI in any meaningful terms: 'It's about looking after the welfare of pupils while simultaneously introducing trainees to professional practices, to help them in personal growth and professional development, as classroom practitioners'. Those mentors who did refer to the HEI when defining their role did so in order to distinguish the HEI's contribution to training from that of the mentor: 'The mentor gives all they've done in college a practical dimension'.

Mentors cited three sources for their understanding of the role: common sense and experience, the school, and the HEI. All but one mentor cited the influence of the HEI but all gave more weight to the other two sources in defining their understanding of their role. It was apparent that lip-service was being paid to the role of the provider institution but that this paled into insignificance when compared with common sense and the experience of supervising students. Mentors typically defined the HEI's contribution in this area in rather cursory terms, which at times bordered on the disparaging, before moving on to the other two sources which were then described expansively: 'There was an in-service training day but it comes from understanding something of human nature. It's common sense knowing what students need. The professional mentor played an important part too'. This response was typical in stressing the importance of experience and common sense: 'It's in part common sense. We've been doing it for years. It's something English teachers do anyway; we tend to be supportive of each other'. 'It's common sense, based upon our own experience of what we were taught and not taught'.

When asked to pinpoint the individual, whether from the HEI or the school, who had been most influential in defining their role, mentors unhesitatingly and without exception referred to the professional mentor. Only two mentors described the HEI curriculum tutor as having any influence; two mentioned the PGCE course director as having some influence and two referred to the minor influence of 'documents', without being able to ascribe authorship. One mentor spoke for the majority when he stated: 'Ninety-five per cent of the influence in defining my role has come from the school; only 5 per cent from the university. After all we only see the subject tutor two or three times throughout the year so the influence from the university is bound to be very limited'.

When questioned about the perception of others of their role, it became apparent that the majority of the mentors had never been confronted with this issue. Some charted views which had changed over time: 'The department perceived it negatively at first but now feel more positive as they see the benefits. We've been a flagship in the school and so the status of the department has risen accordingly'. 'It was originally viewed as quite an appealing job since most of the department wanted to supervise students. But now the department recognizes that times have changed and that the role of the mentor is a demanding one'.

Only one mentor unequivocally described the department's response as being very supportive. All those mentors who fulfilled other managerial roles, whether as head of department, second in department or as a senior teacher, felt that other staff perceived mentoring as merely an extension of those responsibilities. Responses regarding the headteacher's perception of the mentor's role were mixed. While five mentors reported that the headteacher's attitude was very supportive, several felt that the headteacher would not be aware of the mentoring role and one could only conjecture: 'He might implicitly judge that my selection by the professional mentor was a sign that I was considered competent'.

## Rewards and Compensation

Half the mentors questioned stated that they had not anticipated and had not been promised any personal rewards or compensation for taking on the role. None of these had subsequently been rewarded or compensated in any way whatsoever. Of the remainder, one mentor had been promised reward 'through an enhanced curriculum vitae and professional development' but did not feel that this was an adequate recompense. One mentor's only 'reward' had been free membership of the university library and another was initially promised protected time 'but this never materialized because of pressure from the timetable and staff absence'. Another, equally resigned, mentor was originally promised financial reward, 'but having done one year unpaid, it just continued in that way'. However, this was the only mentor to consider that the time freed because an associate teacher was taking his lessons constituted a reward in itself, but only where the associate was competent: 'a weak student costs time'. Another mentor was informed that she did not deserve protected mentoring time since the associate teacher freed time through teaching her classes. The mentor had objected vigorously but had since received no concessions. One mentor had received vague promises of 'a sum of money' but had received nothing. Another had been promised payment, received nothing but remained hopeful that the promise would be kept. Only one mentor of those promised financial reward had been paid, 'from the school fund'. In only one case was financial reward for mentoring given unequivocally to the English department (a sum of £650). In another case the department had been told that they would have to split the £250 received with the school fund. One department had received a lap-top computer from the school as a quid pro quo for accepting an associate teacher.

Those questioned held strong views as to how mentors should be rewarded. However, there was no consensus concerning how this should be achieved. Four mentors felt that they should be compensated personally through additional free time and through a financial allowance. Eight mentors felt that it was time that was significantly lacking, rather than funding, and of these four considered that granting the mentor an additional payment was potentially divisive: 'Mentoring is very much a shared departmental responsibility. For one person to receive payment would seem unfair. It would unsettle relationships if I was paid. But no one would begrudge me extra time'. 'Financial reward for the mentor creates difficulties since it could lead to confrontation. It's time that's the issue. If the role of the mentor is to be a developing one, then protected time must be built in, in advance'.

Of the eight mentors who felt that additional time was needed, three considered that the extent of this need was in large part determined by the calibre of the associate teacher: 'The time question is so related to the quality of the student. If the student's doing well there are time advantages for the mentor, but it's a very different matter where the student is having difficulties'. 'Time is in very short supply for helping weak students. The professional mentor asked for protected free time from the senior management team but he has been unsuccessful. I may well abandon mentoring if we get another weak student, particularly since mentoring is not well rewarded'.

It was clear from all the responses that, irrespective of whether rewards or time compensation had been received, mentors had originally volunteered for or accepted the role for reasons which had nothing to do with reward and far more to do with more altruistic concerns, typified by this response: 'We must be involved in training the English teachers of the future. We owe it to the profession'. However, it was clear that a creeping realization of the time commitment and skills involved, coupled sometimes with the disillusionment engendered by an occasional weak associate teacher, and sometimes with the recognition that the school was profiting from the delegation of HEI funds, had made mentors more determined that the role should be rewarded, particularly through protected time.

The mentors were aware of the financial anomalies endemic in a system in which each school autonomously decided whether and how to reward its mentors. Half the mentors reported practices in other schools which differed from those in their own, even though they were allied in the same partnership scheme. Even where other mentors were receiving preferential rewards, there was no sign of resentment in the responses of the English mentors: 'In other schools mentors have received cheques. I wouldn't want that'. 'Some schools have allocated scale points, and others have given funds for resources, which seems a good idea'. The remaining half of the sample had no knowledge of how other schools were rewarding mentors and did not appear keen to uncover this information.

Mentors' responses indicated that the diverse and confused reward pattern, perhaps predictably, extended to the ways in which decisions were made concerning these rewards. When asked to confirm who decided how and when they should or should not be rewarded, all 12 mentors made a significantly distinctive response concerning the personnel involved and whether or not the rationale for the decision had ever been explained: 'The senior management team made the decision. They haven't provided a rationale: they're still arguing about it'. 'The appropriate deputy head made the decision informally when discussing the matter with the head of English. The deputy said that he didn't see any reason why the department shouldn't get the money'. 'Initially all the mentors voted that we should not be paid but now we've realized the toll that mentoring takes we've voted for personal payment. However, nothing's materialized yet'.

Mentors were not quick to condemn the ways in which decisions had been reached, despite the fact that so few had received any direct reward, compensation or any indirect benefits through grants to departments. There was a sense of resignation at worst rather than objection, a general feeling of, 'this is how things are done' and in some cases signs of surprise that any interest should be taken in this issue. It was clear that mentors were being asked to consider areas which had not been confronted in any detail in school nor in meetings with HEI tutors.

## Benefits and Disadvantages

While mentors reported that their role had generally gone unrecorded, and almost entirely so in personal terms, they were well aware of the potential benefits they had initially anticipated that the role would bring, both to themselves and to their departments. Associate teachers were seen as a significant stimulus for the mentor's own development and appraisal: 'I felt it would broaden my experience. In explaining ideas to others you have to clarify these issues for yourself and that is particularly important in English teaching'. 'I saw having students as a form of appraisal for me, in meeting the new ideas and initiatives that a student can bring'.

All the mentors stressed the considerable benefits for the department from accepting associate teachers who would introduce fresh ideas and approaches. A number of responses implicitly ascribed an importance to trainees as communicators of ideas, which would more normally be provided through in-service courses: 'Students come with new ideas; they bring a freshness and an enthusiasm. There's a lot of jaded teachers in schools. They give us a boost'. 'Students are the new blood of the profession. They bring new ideas and the exchange of resources'.

Three mentors commented on the potential benefits of having an extra member of staff in the department: 'Students should lead to a lessening of work for all of us. They can also introduce new ideas to members of the department who are in a bit of a rut'. When questioned about the anticipated benefits of mentoring for their pupils, mentors typically returned to the notion of youth and initiative: 'It's good for them to have a change of face and someone young with good ideas'. All but two mentors confirmed that their expectations of the benefits of mentoring had been largely realized. These two blamed their university departments of education and specifically recorded a disillusionment with what they saw as an unequal partnership: 'I expected more from the university. I hoped that the role of mentor would be more clearly defined. The university stressed that the role of mentor was very important. We expected more documentation and more visits from the university subject tutor'. 'I feel the university hasn't delivered its part of the bargain and won't do while we barely see the subject tutor in the building'.

When asked whether they had been fully aware at the outset of the implications of taking on the role, six of the mentors stated that the time commitment had been greater than envisaged. However, other mentors' responses were more sanguine: 'Perhaps I wasn't absolutely sure of how the role had changed but I was pleased to find that I was required to do what I'd always done before mentoring started'.

It became clear that the problems mentors had experienced fell largely into the 'time' and 'administration' categories: 'I lost lunch times, after school time and free periods to student counselling'. 'It's difficult ensuring that pupils are not taught by too many students'. 'Students can be costly in photocopying terms'.

Elsewhere, mentors were quick to transform their responses into positives, typically beginning replies with, 'Perhaps that was a problem initially but...'. Where problems had arisen, mentors were quick to mitigate, seeing trainees as having to cope with demands which caused problems for more experienced teachers: 'Some pupils misbehave with a student but this is inevitable, particularly in a quite difficult school like ours'. Mentors typically identified some problems associated with pupil behaviour and National Curriculum and department record-keeping, but characteristically saw these as predictable and resolvable minor costs of an arrangement where the benefits were significantly greater: 'Pupils try it on with a new face but they do it with anyone new, including us at the beginning of a new year'. 'Students can have some problems with record-keeping but it can be helpful to have a different perspective from our own'. 'Pupils' work rate was initially slower than with me but this was remedied by the end of the practice'.

Mentors described a process of amelioration over time as they grew into the role, the department learned to accommodate the mentoring process and as associate teachers' skills developed: 'The time question and the department problems eased. I became better at time management and another member of staff is going to become a mentor, which has removed some of the department barriers'. The lack of time was identified as the most intractable problem of all those associated with mentoring: 'Time's the most insoluble problem. I can't see that this will improve, rather than the opposite. The expectations of mentors will increase rather than decrease'.

Mentors clearly found it easier to describe the benefits rather than the problems associated with mentoring and did so expansively. Three-quarters of those questioned outlined the significant enhancement to the curriculum offered by associate teachers. Mentors saw the benefits in this area as either direct, through the 'freshness' that associate teachers introduced or indirect, in jolting the mentor into a reappraisal of the curriculum offered: 'The enthusiasm he brought into his lessons offered a further extension of the curriculum and variation within it'. 'Having students allows more time for reviewing the curriculum. Discussing content and approaches with a student is probably the only time I discuss English teaching since department meetings are dominated by "business"'.

Where pupil achievement was concerned, mentors felt that the temporary impact of deteriorating pupil behaviour, which was generally resolved over time, was compensated for by significant benefits: 'With two teachers in the room you're able to spend more time with pupils with particular needs and this brings benefits for achievement and behaviour all round'. 'In many cases pupils responded very well to a particularly interesting scheme of work, produced with great care by a student'. 'Our pupils have benefited considerably – academically – from having students'. One mentor spoke for the majority in describing the beneficial impact of enjoyment on pupil behaviour and achievement: 'The key benefit is pupil *enjoyment*. Our pupils have really enjoyed having students in. Their achievement in group work and oral work has improved significantly. We teach in a fairly traditional way here and students provide interesting activities and deal with issues in a contemporary way'.

Three-quarters of the mentors identified significant benefits related to time in having associate teachers working within the department. They included, with one exception, all those who had expressed particular concern about the lack of time for adequate mentoring: 'Staff feel they have more time for curriculum development, for assessment, and for background reading'. 'We couldn't have completed moderation so effectively without having students teaching our classes'. 'Having her freed me from lesson planning and teaching even though I continued to monitor her work'.

Thus it would appear that while mentoring can cause particular problems for mentors whose time for counselling associate teachers is not protected, there are more general time benefits for the mentor and department staff in having an associate teacher who will free time, and that these benefits increase as the trainee gains in competency. A picture emerges of the need for an investment in safeguarded counselling time throughout the school experience but particularly during the early induction stages, and of the increasing return on this investment as the associate teacher and teaching practice progress. This pay-off is of course threatened where the practice is so short that it barely moves beyond induction.

With one exception, all the mentors emphasized the beneficial impact of associate teachers on department resources. They were seen as improving these through prompting a reappraisal and through introducing their own novel resources: 'Having students activates a wider range of resources. For example, a student may use a neglected resource or bring in a new one, and discussion with a student will introduce new approaches to the resources we commonly use'. All mentors identified significant advantages in having associate teachers as aides in the assessment process. They were seen as helpful in freeing time for more experienced teachers to assess pupils more comprehensively, in encouraging reappraisal and in joining in the assessment process, sometimes almost as equals: 'Having two adults facilitates certain types of assessment. We can back up each other's judgement'. 'He brought in pieces of pupils' work which we related to our own "cold" department document on assessment. It made us reassess its usefulness'.

An invitation to place the benefits in rank order of importance prompted mentors to sum up, often powerfully, their views of the important personal and departmental benefits of mentoring associate teachers. Whatever concerns they had expressed earlier, particularly about the workload and lack of time, mentors seemed sure of the advantages, which can be grouped into three main categories: staff development, enhancement of the curriculum, and freeing of staff. These responses were confirmed in mentors' statements concerning their own current attitudes to mentoring which were, with one exception, essentially very positive. Any qualifications invariably related to the lack of time to fulfil the role appropriately: 'It's very rewarding as you see a student develop and gain in confidence, and as you see pupils benefit. The only negative aspect is that it's very time-consuming'. 'There are days when I feel that it's not worth all the time commitment but I still feel that students are in the right place. It's teachers and schools experiences which will make them into teachers. It's rewarding and over all a very good experience'. 'The role of mentor is a thoroughly enjoyable one: rewarding and a challenge'.

## Attitudes

Only one mentor of the 12 interviewed stated that she was equivocal about continuing in the role. However, this was because of anticipated possible problems caused by a confluence of lack of time and a poor associate teacher: 'I can see the real benefits for myself, the department and for the pupils but there's also the time element. I would have to have time set aside to do the job properly'. Five of the mentors were prepared to state that their own positive attitudes regarding mentoring were reflected by their departments. However, the remainder were either unsure of their departments' views or felt they were equivocal and highly dependent on the calibre of associate: 'They feel they have a responsibility for training the next generation of English teachers but generally they don't understand what the role of mentor is'. 'They'd say its wonderful when we've had good students but that it's a nightmare when we've had a weak one'.

When asked what changes, if any, they would like to see introduced by their partner HEIs in order to support their role, three-quarters of the mentors advocated more visits from the curriculum tutor and several mentors stated that, without this support, the concept of partnership was flawed since schools were being asked to carry too much of the burden of ITE: 'We'd like to see subject tutors from the college coming into school more often so that they can see how the *school* functions. Students need to see and relate to the subject tutor too'. 'Since we have to pass and fail students now we need the reassurance of subject tutors coming in more, not less. Every group the student teaches ideally should be seen by the tutor'.

Three mentors advocated improved training, two emphasized the value of subject-specific mentor meetings, one called for more consistent management by the HEI and one for a review of the documentation required. Only one mentor advocated more funding reaching the school as payment for the training of associate teachers.

Finally, when asked whether they felt that English mentors had distinctive qualities which set them apart from other subject mentors, all but two of the sample stated that they felt that the particular nature of 'English' set English teachers and thus mentors apart from their colleagues: 'English teachers are special because their subject is less content-based. Other subjects have textbooks in a way which we don't. Our students are more adventurous and have more personality. They're generally self-confident, articulate people and you need confidence to teach English'. 'We're special because we have the most demanding subject to teach. We're the most open to criticism, misunderstanding and ignorance. We *must* have a clear theoretical basis for our teaching in order to do it with confidence and defend it with confidence'.

## The Future

This survey confirms that those mentors interviewed derived much personal and professional benefit from mentoring English associate teachers and that these benefits are perhaps particularly welcomed by mentors who are members of stable and middle-aged departments which are in need of new perspectives and new blood. It would appear that the mentors surveyed will continue to appreciate the value of associate teachers who can help to revitalize sometimes jaded staff and reinvigorate teaching methodologies. However, this assessment of the worth of associate teachers was, predictably, heavily dependent on the calibre of the associates and those who had experience of a weak one had clearly been very disillusioned. Should the general quality of applicants for teacher training fall, as might occur at a time of more buoyant employment prospects elsewhere, then it is possible that these mentors and many more would have cause to reassess their attitude to trainees, particularly if HEI expectations of mentors continue to rise.

The future of ITE is precariously dependent on the goodwill of mentors, the 'silent majority' in partnerships which may be in danger of paying lip-service to their importance without recognizing this in any meaningful way. It is difficult to foresee how a system of school-based teacher training can be sustained long term when, if this sample is typical, those who are most influential in supporting and assessing associate teachers in schools are so clearly unrewarded and unsupported by the HEI, their schools and, surprisingly, by their own departments in many cases. Personal financial rewards would appear to be less of an issue at a time when these English mentors, at least, still have sufficient personal investment in mentoring to sustain them in their role. However, if protected mentoring time is not guaranteed and as mentors become more acutely aware of the anomalous nature of the reward system, it is easy to foresee mentors making escalating demands for payment. It is perhaps significant that in the two schools in the sample in which mentors had formed a distinctive group, these more radical demands were already being voiced.

For the majority of mentors in this sample the notion of partnership, in which ITE is currently embedded, was almost meaningless. Partnership had provided them with training which was generally seen as inconsequential, had denied them any significant role in course management or the selection of associate teachers, and had led to almost no contact with the HEI tutor whose support and guidance they valued most. It would seem that resources will have to be found so that HEI curriculum tutors can spend more time in partnership schools, working with mentors and students, if they are to convince English mentors, at least, that partnership is a worthwhile entity.

In recent years, 'empowerment' has become a key term when documenting mentors' contributions to ITE. This is usually taken to refer to mentors' confidence in understanding and competently fulfilling their partnership role. Ironically, those mentors in the survey felt 'empowered' through common sense and experience to mentor their associate teachers adequately, but this legitimization of their role would not and could not be one that the HEI could endorse, given its implication that nothing much had changed and that formal training was redundant. However, these mentors were not stating that they felt empowered to go it alone. There was no indication that mentors wanted schools to have sole responsibility for training teachers; quite the opposite. There was a significant call for more subject-specific mentor meetings as a potentially valuable form of ongoing training and a repeated plea for support through more frequent visits from curriculum tutors.

A picture of a range of partnerships, which are seen as being both peculiar and contradictory, emerges from the responses of these mentors. While the seven HEIs involved seem to control the course structure, certainly so in the perceptions of these mentors, the schools – individual autonomous institutions – crucially selected their own mentors in a variety of ways, for which coherent rationales were seldom provided, least of all to the mentors. It is a truism that any school-based system of ITE that cannot ensure quality of mentoring cannot guarantee overall course quality and yet these mentors' responses indicate that, in their partnerships at least, a key element in quality assurance was being decided at times almost by default. It is difficult to see, given the dwindling nature of mentor training, exacerbated by the lack of HEI funds to support this, how provider institutions can claim to guarantee course quality when they, like the mentors themselves, are in no position to ensure consistent and coherent mentor selection procedures and rewards.

## Conclusions

These findings do not differ markedly from those considered earlier, particularly in Chapters 3 and 4; if anything they reveal a sample with greater commitment and less concern for rewards than the general cohort. The recruitment, training and reward issues previously detailed are evident concerns within the English departments investigated. However, this work has shown how a particular curriculum area can gain as a result of associate participation and how departmental revitalization might be enhanced as involvement is planned, resourced and evaluated. Whether there is any variation between the requirements of subject areas in the acquisition of competence and experience, and hence a suitability or otherwise for a mentoring approach, is a matter for further investigation. However, the commitment and readiness to develop opportunities shown by the mentors interviewed suggest that the subject has made particular gains where associates have been seen as a positive resource rather than a drain on the staff involved.

*Chapter 8*

# Interaction and Impact

*Derek Glover and Gerry Gough*

The case study evidence charts the complexity of the interaction of the partners in the teacher education process within schools as dynamic communities that are caught in a tension between a variety of external pressures and their own strategic needs. The reference from time to time to 'feeling that we want to take associates in more departments but we have to be so careful that we don't take on anything that gets in the way of our eventual results', reflects a will to help that is frustrated by the need for schools to continue to do well in those aspects of their work which are judged by the public and which might affect pupil recruitment. We have been able to consider how the staff and management teams of individual schools, professional and subject mentors, others in the subject departments and the associates themselves have reacted to an evolving situation.The evidence from individual schools shows that, faced with a variety of demands, some schools have not accorded initial teacher education a high priority but have attempted to 'live with it as best we can'.

Because of the differing importance attached to participation in initial teacher education, some schools are more ready to receive associates then others. In the practical application of virtually all the aspects of mentoring examined in the previous chapters there is a range between those schools where staff have thought about the needs of the new role and developed a common staff philosophy and practice for associates, and those where mentoring as an additional activity is seen as a means of earning extra funds with only limited effort. Even so, staff have had to deal with the practical issues and negotiate roles and responsibilities within the organization and in partnership with the HEIs. There is considerable evidence that this work has been helped or hindered because of the existence of a generally positive or negative department or school environment for initial teacher education. Both the qualitative and quantitative evidence shows that virtually all

135

elements of the training experience appear to exist at some point along a continuum of philosophy and organization from the supportive to the adverse within each school or college. These elements can be grouped to present a picture of the training environment. Our contention is that the attitudes of subject mentor, the subject department, and the school as a cultural whole, may determine the eventual success of mentoring for both associates and pupils.

## Subject Mentors

The recruitment, training and retention of mentors appears to play a major part in determining the effectiveness of the training for individual associates. In some schools and college departments, mentoring occurs because traditionally a member of staff has been responsible for associates in training within a department. There is then a range of practice, often with increasing commitment, to those schools where mentoring has been offered as an additional post and applications have been invited from staff who have then been selected with procedures of varying rigour. It may also happen that a person becomes a mentor because there was nobody else to undertake the task or because the allocation of tasks within a department is balanced through undertaking the mentoring responsibility. The impact of this upon mentoring commitment owes much to the priorities accorded to the role by the individual concerned.

Once appointed, mentors are then offered training of varying content and quality. This may emphasize developmental support for students (as in Vonk, 1993), or it may be more concerned with the procedures necessary to ensure that there is consistency in the treatment of all associates on a course. Support, assessment and development require additional time input by mentors, especially where the associate has problems which may necessitate constant attention. However, rewards for this time are often lost because of variations in the way in which resources allocated for mentoring are distributed. Not surprisingly, and compounded by the personal and professional pressures which a mentor may be experiencing, commitment, motivation and attitude to the associate may be variously affected. The range of expertise is shown in the following contrasted associates' comments: 'My mentor was really concerned to help me succeed'. 'The mentor at the school could have helped more and given much more support... they are there to help us so that we can help them by the end of the practice'.

# The Subject Department

The associate usually works in a subject area in which several other teaching and non-teaching staff are involved. The other staff may be involved either by providing training opportunities or simply by supporting the work undertaken within the department. At its extreme, we have evidence from our study of an associate at one school being denied access to observe a textiles technology lesson because the mentor, a home economist, was the person paid to undertake the work, but we have also found several examples of a shared departmental possession referring to 'our student'. It is not only in its general atmosphere but in the overall attitude to the provision of resources and the opening-up of training experiences that a department can affect associate development.

Gitlin (1987) has argued that within the close working group which a secondary subject department usually becomes, associates will be affected by corporate involvement in curriculum making and implementation, the development of the skills of effective teaching, teacher relationships, and the nature of teacher-associate relations. Our evidence suggests that this organizational context of the mentoring activity may also have a supportive or inhibiting influence on associate satisfaction. If mentoring is seen to be a high-status activity within the department, in the eyes of one head of department, 'because it gives us a close and continuing link with the university which we use to advantage with the senior students', the department as a group may give more material and personal support to the associates. At one extreme, one associate reports, 'I had strong encouragement from the departmental staff', but another comments, 'I do not feel the department at my school was a good place to do the main practice; they were not interested in the associate training scheme and as a result I was left in a sink-or-swim situation'.

## The School

The atmosphere for training engendered by the school may be influenced by a range of variables. At Portland School, the professional mentor summed up the staff aim for the inclusion of associates in their community: 'Associates are not a nuisance to be endured...they are additional members of staff who ought to be welcomed as people who are able to help the regular teaching staff with their primary task of providing the best possible, and most enjoyable, education for the youngsters it is possible to manage'. The factors which affect the nature of the school environment for associates include the attitudes of the senior management team, however designated, and referred to by one associate as a 'group of people who were far too busy to have time for the associates who they felt got in the way'; but who at one school have developed a code for the incorporation of associates into school life. At a more practical level there is also evidence that some associates may be denied access to resources or may have to 'exist as second-class citizens when seeking help in the office'.

Where associates are seen as a necessary evil, managed, but not developed, by a professional mentor who is a member of a hard-pressed senior team without either time or recognition for the liaison work necessary, the attitude of the school staff as a whole tends to see the activity as an additional burden, often with limited empathy or support for the training process. Where the associates are accepted as part of a whole school policy, and where this work is integrated with the general professional development of staff, our evidence is of positive and productive relationships. The case study evidence shows that there is a more positive environment where all staff are working towards common standards of classroom management and mutual respect. This enables the associate to be more rapidly assimilated into the school and allows mentoring to be a successful activity. At Orchard school, a five form entry mixed 11–16 comprehensive school, the assimilation of ten associates has been welcomed as a way forward in the development of team approaches, individualized learning programmes, and staff development. Associate experience is reflected as follows: 'The school was really good, with helpful staff who seemed to want us to be part of things'. At another school, however, the experience was much more negative for an associate who commented, 'At the school there was no real support, evaluation or assessment...valuable in terms of learning to survive but not in enhancing my confidence or self-esteem'.

# Interaction

The combined impact of the attitude of the subject mentor and the other members of the department, and interaction between associates and staff within the department and the school, is the basis of a mentoring culture within a school. Mentor, department and school as elements in the mentoring environment can act in ways which are supportive of the associate, or they can be unhelpful and negative in a way which he or she considers to be counter-productive. Training experiences which are developed by the mentor, department and school as part of a consistent and positive policy permit the process of induction and progression towards professional competence (Leithwood, 1992; Ryan, 1986). We recognize, though, that in a minority of placements there may be personality mismatches on the part of either associate or mentor which intensify the structural effects of the mentoring environment. For example David, who as a mature associate believed that only a didactic approach could succeed, was not prepared to act on the requirements of his mentor that he should vary his teaching strategies, was critical of others in the department who suggested alternative classroom management techniques, and reported to the course director that there was no rapport between himself and a 'disorganized, progressive mob'. Within the same department and school, and at the same time, Clare was outstandingly successful.

# The Training Environment

There is a range of descriptions which can be applied to mentor, department and school, extending from the supportive which encourages the associate and opens up training opportunities, to the adverse which is inclined to inhibit experiential activity and to limit the training potential of the practice. Our evidence, related to the work of Stoll (1992) and Loder (1990), and drawn from interview responses, indicates that there are broadly-based recognizable descriptors for each element in the total training environment. These provide a framework for understanding and analysis of the training process. The two extremes are as shown in Table 8.1 which attempts to characterize supportive and adverse mentor, department and school behaviour and attitude.

**Table 8.1** *Elements of the training environment*

| | Supportive | Adverse |
|---|---|---|

**Mentor**

| | | |
|---|---|---|
| | Good role model with good knowledge of subject, challenging teaching style, good pupil and staff relationships, sympathetic but firm manner, insistence on standards, follows procedures and shows loyalty to others, commitment in time and effort, enjoyment of communication and counselling and monitoring activity, sees the associate as a personal responsibility | Poor role model with limited knowledge of subject, pedestrian teaching style, abrasive pupil and staff relationships, withdrawn or cynical, sloppy in procedures, ready to blame others, has little time for associate, sees work as a chore, little contact with associate except when required by crisis or formal procedures |

**Department**

| | | |
|---|---|---|
| | Team approach strong, see associate(s) as part of the team, share responsibility, assess the part each might play in support, evaluate on a regular basis, include the associate in activities, share in planning and providing opportunities, not concerned about fee arrangements | Function on an individual basis, see associates as mentor's sole responsibility, not ready to cooperate in support, no part in planning or evaluation, see associate as a nuisance but do as requested by mentor but no more, regard the mentor as paid for the job |

**School**

| | | |
|---|---|---|
| | Has a strong system of shared values with whole school professional development and ITE policy known and understood, associates welcomed and integrated developing professionalism recognized, valued as a source of new ideas and professional help, support in all aspects of personal and professional growth, active in links with HEI staff, build upon the development of competence and confidence | Accept associates as a source of income but little common warmth, ITE seen as bolt-on activity, associates marginalized in staff room, recognition of associate problems as arising from deficiencies of partnership management, belief in old-style apprenticeship, tendency to denigrate HEI support, may be critical of associates in front of pupils or other staff |

In discussion of this model with associates, there was a view that the impact of the mentor upon the development, of confidence and competence was more important than that of the department, unless the mentor was of poor quality when the associate would be likely to turn to another member of the department for help. Similarly the impact of the department was ranked above that of the school because it would be unlikely that an associate would look beyond his or her own subject area for help and support but would nevertheless be 'susceptible to the atmosphere of the place and ready to turn to others for help if necessary'. This, of course, varies with the personality of the associate and the opportunities in an individual placement. The descriptors in the model do represent points on a continuum and can all be neutral in their effect on the individual associate teacher. This may occur where the mentor allows the associate to develop his or her own style without active involvement; where the department accepts, but does not foster the associate; and where the staff of the school similarly acknowledge but do not positively welcome their teacher education role. Those closest to the associate have the most influence on the mentoring environment, especially where the experience is of short duration, or where the placement is in a large institution such as a tertiary college. Interview evidence suggests that the influence of the school culture is actually quite strong, 'because it makes a difference to the attitudes of the staff room and if that is generally warm and welcoming, then everything else seems to go right'.

While normally the ranking of influence declines from that of the mentor, to the other members of the department, and thence to the staff of the school, this may be changed because of personalities, local circumstances and the particular local organizational issues of an interpersonal nature which might cloud the readiness to receive and support associates. James had a shared mentorship between three members of the maths department, but because he felt that they were a powerful team to whom he could not disclose his problems, he turned to other members of the school staff for support through physical and social education team activities. Mandy had excellent formal mentor support but the mentor as head of department was often preoccupied and the support and influence she needed on a day-to-day basis came from the two younger members of the department. Mark felt that his experience was inhibited because one of the department had been made compulsorily redundant in an atmosphere of mistrust and recrimination.

The influence of mentors may be tempered by the other responsibilities they carry, by their age and length of time in teaching, by their attitude to change, and by their professional commitment and aspirations. The department may be a micropolitical arena into which the associate has unwittingly strayed. The impact on the associate is greatest if he or she works with more than one member of staff, and if attitudes reflect a commonality of purpose and a team spirit or the antithesis of this in a group which suspects the motivation and is overtly critical of the practices of colleagues. The influence of the school is yet more complex and appears to be related to the age and social structure of the staff, the folklore of past associate experience, shared loyalty, and the degree of willingness to open up activities and discussions to comparative strangers. In short, the complexity of influences is considerable and the viewpoint often subjective. Overall, there is a variation from 58 per cent to 93 per cent associate satisfaction with their experience classified by subject area as shown in the 1994 associate PGCE evaluation. Contributing factors to this are illustrated in Table 8.2, which summarizes the questionnaire responses which were linked to the motivation of associates to continue teaching (often school-related), the way in which they felt that they had been prepared within schools (often department-related), and the nature of the mentor support they received.

**Table 8.2** *Associate satisfaction with subject experiences (%)*

| Feature | Physics | English | Maths |
| --- | --- | --- | --- |
| Motivation to teach | 87.5 | 77.6 | 71.7 |
| Preparation in school | 84.3 | 70.2 | 70.7 |
| Mentor support | 74.6 | 69.0 | 56.0 |

Discussion with mentors about this data suggests that the physicists may feel more satisfied because 'their conversion from traditional science to newer integrated approaches means that we just have to work with them', and the mathematicians less supported within the schools and by mentors because of the use of structured courses which 'build upon what is done by the class teacher but don't require the close contact that is needed in some other subjects'. Such comments indicate that there may be a wide variation in the degree of support by both school and HEI staff traditionally accorded to different subject areas.

## The Reality

Although cautious because of the the inexactness of our data and the subjectivity of viewpoints, we suggest that the training environments as a cultural totality may be identified as being broadly supportive, neutral or adverse for the associate. This may be illustrated from the experience of associates within three of the case study environments.

At Greenfield, a large college of further education, associates placed within the economics department are fostered by a mentor who has been teaching for eight years, who has a good rapport with both associates and the HEI, and who has an easy while at the same time demanding relationship with people, and supporting high standards. This supportive environment is minimized within the department of seven who see the associates as an additional responsibility undertaken by the mentor who gets an additional number of hours for the work. In consequence, there is very limited contact and a neutral impact. Even more adverse is the view of the general studies staff as a whole, who constitute the nearest within the college to a school unit, and who regard the associates as likely to impede the drive being undertaken by the department to ensure positive 'league table' achievement.

At Kingsland, a four form entry 11–16 rural comprehensive school, there are ten associates placed as five pairs with five mentors. The fee income is split, with one third going to the mentors, one third to the departments and one third retained by the school to pay for the work undertaken by the professional mentor and to supplement school resources likely to be used by the staff as a whole. The decision to take associates had been made by the staff as a whole who have negotiated a payback in participation in professional development programmes offered by the college. In a school where departments are small and personnel interlinked, where the pupils are used to a fairly open system with classroom assistants, associates and volunteers all working in team situations, the associates are welcomed, integrated and supported. In the one case where there were poor relationships between one of a pair of associates and the mentor, contingency money has been used to pay the other member of the department to act as an alternative, and successful mentor. All three elements are seen to be more or less supportive.

A similar situation exists at Wake school, where the departmental staff are supportive of associates and the school staff as a whole welcome additional help during the training periods. However, within one subject area the mentor insists on undertaking the task although as head of a major faculty he finds it difficult to find time for the associates. He will only allocate associates to the non-exam years and the low attaining groups, despite pressure from his colleagues, and believes strongly in staff presence at all times when associates are teaching. This mentoring environment might be described as neutral because the associates are supported by others in the faculty, but in reality it is an adverse situation for the associate concerned because all his colleagues within the school have a totally supportive environment within which to develop.

Our evidence points, therefore, to the possibility that it is the summative effect of the interaction between mentor, department and school which will determine the impact of training experience upon the associate. If an attempt is made to systematize the impact of influences on teacher education, the following taxonomy emerges. Where M=mentor, D=department and S=school, the patterns shown in Table 8.3 may be considered.

**Table 8.3** *Interaction of training elements*

| Nature of elements | | Total training character of placement | Environment |
| Supportive | Adverse | | for associate |
| --- | --- | --- | --- |
| M+D+S | None | Committed, effective, staff development priority | Supportive |
| M+D | S | Departmental strength despite school indifference | Supportive |
| M+S | D | Attempts to change isolated departmental attitudes | Supportive |
| M | D+S | Mentor often working alone and against odds | Neutral |
| D+S | M | Other staff support to replace mentor | Neutral |
| D | M+S | Supportive department ineffectual against traditionalism | Adverse |
| S | M+D | Supportive school inhibited by hostile department attitude | Adverse |
| None | M+D+S | No support, student alone against the system | Adverse |

## Policy Implications

It is our contention that the application of an analysis based upon the taxonomy may point to training and development needs within the system. All case study schools have been subject to negotiated contracts where, in return for a defined training experience, schools and college departments have been paid up to £1,000 per associate placed. The evidence has shown that the process of negotiation has opened the debate within schools and that there are calls for some form of quality assurance in the interests of the associates who are being trained. Much of the folklore about school experience can now be analysed and the impact of the school training situation upon student progress assessed. Recognition that associates are part of the total teaching strength of partnership schools is now acknowledged by headteachers, one of whom commented, 'there is no doubt of the changing situation...classroom mayhem with students is disappearing because our own staff can no longer let insurrection develop, there is a coherent programme agreed with the HEI, and we are realizing that associates can give as well as get whilst they are in the school'. At the same time, some associates feel that 'we don't really belong anywhere because the college hasn't the time or staff to work with us and the school is often too busy to do other than leave us to get on with a minimum of supervision'.

There is a continuing problem in that many HEIs require a large number of places each year, especially where there is a policy of placing only one or two associates in each school. In this situation the development of favourable mentors may be possible within one or two departments, but we found examples of schools where only one or two of the staff had received mentor training and whole school awareness of changed approaches to ITE was limited. Discussion with senior staff in schools indicates that while some would be prepared to allow their staffs to undertake training to raise awareness of effective mentoring, there are strong reservations 'in case this meant that the HEIs then took on some sort of validating role...after all, many of our staff still feel that the college tutors have had it easy in their ivory towers'. It may be that developing contractual arrangements could be directed at an attempt to ensure that mentor, department and school do not develop their teacher training role without a full understanding of the commitment required. The implication of this is seen by one HEI subject tutor as 'the acceptance by the schools of a changed relationship because to get good placements we may need to dictate some of the requirements rather than going cap in hand to find a student-minding opportunity'. From this discussion it emerged that in the total associate experience, awareness of the role of the HEI staff is still of considerable significance. While this role has been affected by the changed time allocations and pedagogic requirements, these staff have played a major part in the training of mentors. Unfortunately, mentor perceptions are that 'it is often nothing more than administrative detail...it is a new situation which the college staff have got to sort out so that our training is about teaching associates to teach'.

From the case studies, the most successful total training environment appears to be that where the school has developed a policy for initial teacher education as part of a total staff development policy, negotiated the payment in time and money as part of a total package for involvement, and where the concept of the training school has become part of the culture. Within one school, the departments are being progressively trained in mentoring skills, the team teaching culture is strong and the assessment process for associates mirrors the appraisal activity within the team. The mentors are then fully trained, and all are pursuing accreditation for the work, the development of a resource base to foster the activity, and prize the weekly time allocation for the work which they are undertaking. The implications of extending this to all training schools are considered in our final chapter.

# References

Gitlin, A D, (1987) 'Common school structures and teacher behaviour', in Smyth, J (ed.) *Educating Teachers: Changing the nature of pedagogical knowledge,* London: Falmer Press.

Leithwood, K A (1992) *Teacher Development and Educational Change*, London: Falmer Press.

Loder, C (1990) *Quality Assurance and Accountability in Higher Education*, London: Kogan Page.

Ryan, K (1986) *The Induction of New Teachers*, Bloomington, IN: Phi Delta Kappa.

Stoll, L (1992) *Teacher Development and Educational Change*, London: Falmer Press.

Vonk, J H C (1993) 'Mentoring beginning teachers: mentor knowledge and skills', *Mentoring*, 1, 1, 31–9.

*Chapter 9*

# The Consequences

*George Mardle*

The aim of this chapter is to examine the consequences of the development of mentoring in relation to an understanding of the appropriate policy and development frameworks which we may begin to promote with regard to teacher education. As indicated previously in Chapter 2, the impetus for change in this area has both a macro policy imperative driven by government as shown in Circular 9/92 and the establishment of the Teacher Training Agency, and a micro dimension arising from the promotion of particular policies as they develop in individual higher education institutions and schools. Our evidence suggests that it would be wrong to assume that those institutions becoming involved in mentoring were purely being reactive. The idea of mentoring and partnership is a proactive process which has a far longer history than responses to present government policy (Wilkin, 1990). What is new is the comprehensive way that *all* institutions in teacher education now have to respond. Yet, as has also been indicated previously, the government has very much left individual institutions to react to these imperatives on an ad hoc and voluntary basis with no real policy guidelines, save for the instruction concerning the proportion of teacher education time spent in schools and that there should be a transfer of financial resources to the schools to cover the work to be undertaken.

The current government concern with a strategic plan for education and a complex and high degree of change to be accomplished at comparative speed has not necessarily detailed the finer points of policy administration. As a consequence, the normal process of pilot programmes, research and evaluation and then the promotion and development of good practice have often been ignored. Some philanthropic organizations, eg, The Paul Hamlyn Foundation, 1994, and The Esmee Fairbairn Charitable Trust, 1995, concerned with the speed of progress and the quality of the product, have sponsored such research programmes in the hope that future developments will be from an informed base of knowledge. The issues explored in this chapter are based upon the work we have undertaken towards understanding all the parameters of the mentoring process.

The basis of the argument is derived from a series of case studies and evidence from two questionnaire surveys. It is, however, important to realize that the use of such case study material, while providing useful and valuable insights into the process, cannot be said to represent any attempt at a total national picture. The material collected does not seek to justify its arguments by reference to any statistical reliability or inferred comparison to a wider population. It is though, the belief of the research team that since the sample taken was of a relatively wide nature, many of the insights available do represent responses, particularly from mentors and schools, which if replicated in other areas would offer similar examples of the issues being faced. The evidence also provides examples of the developing philosophy of partnership involvement and the practical details of changing practices within schools and the HEIs.

In examining the consequences we must therefore be concerned with the variety of levels at which a response is made. In Chapter 1 I argued that the promotion of policy in the development of practice in this area would be the symbiosis of a series of important factors. These would include the response of the staff of the higher education institution; the response of teachers and administrators in the schools; the organizational and structural responses of the schools; the cultural responses of the schools; and finally the interpretation made by all the participants of the ideological and economic climate within which they are working. Importantly, it will be the way in which such responses are articulated and roles combined which will promote the mentoring policy and lead to its embedding in the school situation.

It should also be noted at this stage that the whole process is ongoing. The very speed and nature of change both in education in general and teacher education in particular has often meant quick responses to specific and pressing needs. In one of the HEIs concerned with case study schools, the changes were outlined, developed and agreed with schools in 11 months. In many cases the necessary structural frameworks and the partnership administrative arrangements are only now being fully developed as practices which were known and accepted as part of the traditional framework are challenged, and re-evaluated. Among these, responsibility for the associate assessment is the most frequently mentioned concern, but within two years most schools have accepted that they must have a responsibility for this. The comments of one professional mentor explain this: 'Two years ago I would have said that anything to do with passing and failing should be undertaken by the HEI, but on our advice and evidence...now I regard it as my job and I begin to resent anyone from outside having a say on once-off visits'. So the particular issues addressed are from often new and progressing relationships and practices rather from an established pattern of organization. In short, we offer a snapshot at an early stage of development.

While recognizing that the various components which make up the complex matrix of mentoring cannot be easily separated, it is necessary for analytical purposes to identity more specifically those different elements which appear to impinge upon the inter-relationship. In this regard I intend to begin with the issues expressed by the mentors themselves, outward through the institutional arrangements to a point where the wider policy issues as they are now developing can be addressed. Clearly one way of examining the various components would be to see the arrangement in regard to the variety of advantages and disadvantages which are experienced, and the case study evidence shows that this assessment is being undertaken at all levels. However, that would be to see the process as relatively static, as if the change has already reached some endpoint. Rather, I would wish to argue that what has come out of our research is that particular responses will always depend on a complex amalgam of competing demands and interpretations by the participants themselves as they seek to adapt to, and meet the time needs of, the changed requirements of organization, curriculum and assessment arising from educational change. For many, the view of one mentor summarizes this dilemma: 'it is all a matter of priorities and what I want to do is the best thing for the children I teach...I don't want to do a job which others are better suited to'.

## Mentors and Mentoring

The key element to the whole system is clearly the role and functioning of the mentors themselves. In discussion with one head we learned that 'at the end of the day without the willingness of mentors to undertake the work there would be no training – they have to see that they are gaining something and that they are happy to do the job without detriment to the pupils'.

It could well be argued that as mentors are such an important element in the equation of partnership in teacher education, we should require that individual mentors are motivated, skilled, well trained and able to quickly adopt the role model expected of them. Of course that would tend to assume that such a model was easily identifiable and that teachers could easily fit into it. The reality is far different. Individuals become involved for a variety of complex personal and institutional reasons which range from the genuinely vocational to the purely pragmatic. Two contrasted mentor comments illustrate this: 'I said that I wanted to do the mentoring because it was a way for me to get help with an extra pair of hands in the classroom, as well as give me the fun of supporting somebody who was keen to learn...I felt that it would be better for the kids if I was put on my mettle a bit'. 'I am doing it because we were asked to help and I don't want to let the HEI down, but there is really nothing in it but a lot of work and a few extras for the department'.

In consequence, those involved vary from those who volunteered and who may have been interviewed for the post, to those who were to some extent dragooned into it: 'There is a point where you can't refuse because you want to keep on the right side of the head but when you are in a two-person department and the other one has only been doing the job for a year, to say "yes" means that you are caught'. The position in the hierarchy of the school also varies in that some heads of department wish to keep the reins of power while with others the role is devolved to whom it is seen as most appropriate. Perhaps most importantly, the mentors do not necessarily see themselves as instantaneously good at mentoring even though they were all experienced teachers in the classroom. What they identified was their potential, often based on a view of personal qualities, which would make them effective mentors. Of course all those who become mentors do have, at least initially, plenty of input in the way of training. This provides the basic inputs for the role they will undertake. However, it is clear that the developing role of mentors has yet to be sufficiently articulated and the skills needed fully identified. Our evidence is that the achievement of a standard of coherence in practice and quality in operation is somewhat hit and miss because of the variation in background, motivation and support within the department and the school.

Individual motivation, on the evidence of the material available to us, suggests that those who became mentors were on the whole totally professionally committed, with 76.8 per cent of the respondents believing that the work was stimulating, rewarding and a spur to professional development. Indeed as one mentor expressed the rationale for involvement: 'motivation has to be from the interest in the work and with the students because the money is not a draw'.

Overall, a genuine interest in the development of the next generation of teachers seems of a very high order, with 67.9 per cent of the mentors recognizing their contribution to a shared mentoring culture in the school, and 95 per cent seeing the work as professionally stimulating. The attainment of the qualities for this is summarized in Table 9.1.

**Table 9.1** *Mentor perceptions of professional involvement*

| Qualities gained | % Respondents |
| --- | --- |
| Review and understanding of teaching | 75.1 |
| Better teaching quality | 71.2 |
| Kept up to date | 66.0 |
| Awareness of broader issues | 67.0 |

However, as the financial squeeze on schools and the pressure on teacher salaries increases, with a consequent effect on morale, it may be that this high level of altruism will come under threat. Genuine professional development was also seen as a key motivating factor and in at least a third of the cases, those who volunteered for a mentoring role believed that it would have some value on their cv and might help possible future career development. 'I undertook the training and had an associate with me last year, but this year there was no associate available in my subject at the HEI...in consequence I have lost my chance to continue to develop my skills and I do worry that this might be seen as too brief an involvement when it comes to promotion'. Importantly for those who were not at the level of the head of department, the incentive of career progression was of an extremely high value.

Role definition and expectation also have a clear influence in the work of the mentors and their motivation towards the job. Here the need was for balance between the expectations and frameworks of the higher education institutions and the degree of autonomy sought by the school or the individual within the guidelines given. Most of those involved have seen the initial working of the system in a favourable light and are quickly developing a highly professional model in prac-tice. Indeed there is considerable evidence to suggest that despite teething troubles, the schools and higher education institutions are developing substantial partnership frameworks which allow the coher-ence of the role to develop. While 54 per cent of respondents agreed that the partnership was effective, comment illustrated from one profes-sional mentor suggests that ineffectiveness may be related to matters of administration rather than fundamental difficulty: 'It is a good partner-ship and we get support when we need it – I suppose because we have always worked with the staff of the HEI and know who to call on, but there are some tiresome things like messages not getting through, or two sets of opposed instructions... teething problems, I suspect'.

The point is that without a coherent framework within which mentoring fits, both for the individual and overall within the profession, then there will always be some confusion and disagreement over the precise nature of what is expected. Who should be a mentor, how they should be selected and what is the position of mentoring within the overall profession, are key questions that have so far been answered through the expediency of responses to particular pragmatic impera-tives. Most of the case study material indicates that mentors arrived in their present situation on an unplanned and purely opportunistic basis. The further we move along the road towards mentoring, not only in initial teacher education but also in other aspects of professional devel-opment, the more HEI and school staff need to identify continuity and progression in the process. This will require clear guidelines not only regarding the expectations and requirements of mentoring but also how this fits into the overall scheme of professional and career develop-ment.

Importantly, as mentoring becomes a key aspect of teacher educa-tion and we move towards having a national framework, then the coherence of the system becomes the key issue. There will be, for instance, new mentors becoming involved and others moving to new institutions. How transferable are we to make mentoring? This suggests that a clear framework of mentor accreditation, preferably with some universal recognition, is a must if the overall system is to develop. There is no doubt that the mentors interviewed believed in 'additional training about the why and wherefore of learning within a subject area and about the background to our subject in the curriculum as a whole... thoroughly professional stuff that we need to pass on to those we are looking after', but they did not want 'to go to the HEI at the end of a long day and then listen to a wrangle over how to use the tick boxes'.

To promote effective development of mentoring it needs to be recognized in its own right as part of the *normal* professional development of the teacher. The promotion and development of a 'mentoring culture' with all the potential gains of professional expertise that entails can only be achieved by recognition of the central role of the process in the overall scheme of things. Unfortunately, even at this stage of development, it is clear that schools and higher education institutions have still not necessarily grasped that important nettle. If we are not to see the continuation of the 'bolt-on' process, then clear policies at both local and national level need to be addressed. Our interviews showed that there are still schools where 'we took it on with some misgiving but we knew that if it got too intrusive and the pupils were losing out or it became too much of a chore, we could say enough and pull out'.

## Department/School

In looking at a department within a school or at the whole school and the appreciation of the range and policies of mentoring by senior staff and the staff who may not be mentors, it is often difficult to distinguish between the influence of policy development and personal prejudices in determining attitudes to mentoring. The environments discussed in Chapter 1 have all been seen to a greater or lesser degree within the schools we have been privileged to work with. Yet it is possible to see the core hub of successful mentoring as intrinsically linked to both the department and the school in which it is embedded. The introduction of mentoring to a department, for example, is often done at the level of head of that department. This initially was to be expected in a culture where new innovations which may reflect back into the school structure are relatively sensitive. However, given the pressures that many heads of department feel, particularly because of the demands of the National

Curriculum and assessment, it has become increasingly the case that the work with associates is not undertaken by them. The issue of who should be a mentor then becomes important because the autonomy of the department may be threatened, especially where the professional mentor then negotiates without reference to the head of department. One professional remembers that 'It was like the argument we had in the old days about pastoral care – did we or did we not have to speak to the head of department first...now we might be better able to fit associate needs by not involving a head of department who is opposed to the scheme, but within the department there might be some good staff who have a right to participate and be effective'.

Dependent on a whole range of factors, specifically related to school policies on the issue, a series of tensions might then be created which can ultimately be resolved only at the departmental level. Thus who is selected for mentoring; what time is allocated to mentoring; what resources are available; and how the total experience of those being mentored is organized, can often provide turbulence within a particular department. It was for this reason that at Wake School payment was made totally to those involved as mentors with no sharing of classes, and some of the problems of negotiation with genuinely anxious heads of department avoided.

Yet if there are worries over the difficulties for a department, then there is every possibility that there will also be a great potential for positive input if the work is undertaken. At the crudest level, the input of new recruits in training does provide extra and potentially helpful bodies to the work being done in the department. It furthermore provides an often new and potentially exciting input to the professional work of the staff: 'So far I have looked forward to having a new associate or two with us every year because they generally bring something new or challenge something that I am doing and we get a lot of fun for the youngsters when we do team teaching or group work'. Indeed in the whole equation of costs and benefits to an institution, the role of the associate teacher as a positive resource to the department or school, provided the quality is good, is something that is often overlooked in the general discussions in this area. Concerns at the possible ineptitude or continuing difficulties with unsuitable associates are real where 'we had a bad one a couple of years ago and it will take me a long while to believe that the pupils have actually gained'; the resolution of such difficulties requires positive intervention either by the HEI or other convinced staff.

It is of course at the level of the school that many of these tensions are played out. In essence there are three central issues facing the school overall: first, the level of priority given to its involvement in teacher education; second, the level of financial and resource distribution given to implementing the process; and third, how the management of the process is undertaken.

The level of priority given to teacher education will itself depend on a whole range of factors which may reflect a range of historical influences. These will include the motivation of particular key members of staff, previous relationships with the staff of the HEI, the feelings of the head and the potential role of the process in enhancing the reputation of the school. Even a very positive approach from the senior management team, particularly in the present climate of schools, cannot totally ensure the necessary involvement of staff in any new developments. Thus, at one school previously involved in more traditional arrangements, the head commented: 'we knew that there was some possibility of the system changing and we knew that we had to talk with the staff about things, but we had to be careful because there was a lot of feeling that the work was being done without any pay and since the mid-80s we have learnt that the staff can be touchy'.

From our work there is absolutely no evidence that schools wish to become solely responsible for the entire process, although two of the 20 schools had discussed the possibility of membership of a local training consortium; 'even so, there would have to continue to be some link with the HEI'. Of course one key element in any decision on involvement is that of the effect on the major responsibility of the schools, namely that of educating pupils. As one head put it, the impact of increasing the work of mentoring may: 'put a heavy burden on the schools which, in the interest of the pupils, they may have to consider as an unwanted burden'.

In the light of increased accountability and the enhanced view of parents as customers, this is an important issue. The effect of the burden of initial teacher education can of course be amplified when there is a poor associate teacher or when one particular class is exposed to more than one associate in a given year or over a period of years. Of the 20 schools investigated, one has recognized this to the point of evolving a computer-based system to record associate contact for all pupils, but there is no evidence that these data are used in determining policy.

Many heads of course view the entire process in a very positive light. It enhances the professionalism of the staff, promotes a whole range of particular inputs to the staff development process and provides avenues of staff motivation which allow greater team work in a potentially fragmented structure. Within these schools, staff may still be less happy, especially if the 'potential overcrowding, loss of privacy and the constant awareness that we are in a training situation inhibits the atmosphere of the staffroom'.

Of course the commitment of the head is but one part of the scenario. How far this commitment is then backed up with appropriate support led us to consider the processes and the impact of the resources and time available. While there is no evidence that the school provision of time, resources and money has a direct correlation with the development of mentoring, it is quite clear that successful and quality mentoring does require the input of these variables as it becomes embedded in the school structure. One professional mentor commented: 'when we were at the pilot stage it was sort of feeling our way, but as time has gone on the staff have recognized that they need to be "paid" in some way and they expect that the system will be straightened out in the coming year'. Thus while in the initial development of mentoring there is quite a complex picture, the more the process develops then the more clarity is being required over these areas. For instance it is recognized by many that the time requirements for 'quality mentoring' are not always understood by senior management. The frustration is shown by one mentor who asked, 'Do they really know what it is all about... they think of having a student in as a means of getting free time and they don't seem to want to know what the new job is all about'.

Payment to the school may or may not be transferred to mentors and the distribution of other resources may go in a variety of directions. Clearly in the climate of devolved management it could well be argued that there is a logic to this process and that it is left to each school to act in accordance with its aims and shared values without constraint. However, if we return to the theme of coherence, it is quite clear that discrepancies could have long-term detrimental effects to the whole process. 'Staff talk to each other at the mentor meetings and this is having the effect of bringing about similar practices and policies, but I reckon that those schools which don't actually do something for their staff will quickly lose their support... it isn't that we have to do the job'.

The management of this theme, and the third of our areas of interest, is to some extent the key to the success or otherwise of the other two. Without appropriate management structures to support changed practices and a recognition by the school in terms of its commitment both ideologically and through its allocation of time and resources, then the whole process will fail to function, especially where attempts are made to preserve coherent and quality policies. Evidence would seem to suggest, dependent on the particular circumstances of the school, that either the system is embedded quite quickly into the senior management structure of the school or else the system looks effectively like a bolt-on structure. In the former case, the whole process has to achieve a careful balance between giving the impression of too much centralization while recognizing the significance of having one of the key administrative staff at such a central level, as in the school where 'the professional mentor is the go-between with senior staff and copes with letting them know what we feel and managing a system which is part of the place without intruding'. In the second case, the impression is given that what is expected is just 'another job' which has to be done in reaction to yet another 'immediate pressure' because, as one professional mentor who is also a deputy head comments, 'it is a job I have said I will do for a while and is really not much different from the admin work which I do in other fields'.

Of course having the system located in the framework of the senior management structure does not necessarily mean that the professional tutor, who has overall responsibility for the running of the system, is necessarily a member of that team or that he or she is seen as maintaining responsibility for a vital function of the school.

Overall, then, we have a process which, despite a number of initial problems, is becoming recognized as part of the professional development strategy in many schools, embedded in the school development plan and in some schools it has become linked to the INSET programme and the appraisal process. Increasingly the more the school accepts the advantages of moving towards a 'mentoring culture', the more that process has become part of the school infrastructure. However, a note of caution should be indicated. Not all schools are moving fast and as one deputy head indicated, they did not wish to convey the view 'that we are irretrievably committed to something about which we have serious doubts with the present funding'.

Thus whilst the initial flurry of activity has often held the interest and commitment of schools, there is evidence that as they become more sophisticated in financial and resource management, the harder edge of decision making is coming to the fore. This may explain the early evidence (*Times Educational Supplement,* 1995) that some schools are unwilling to continue their involvement in initial teacher education where the costs in time and staff resources may be detrimental to the organization.

## Associate

One of the most important and interesting aspects of developing a mentoring system is the consequences for those who are in receipt of the programmes, namely the associates. Most evaluative work in this area suggest that a strong involvement with the school is something welcomed by those in training. In the associate evaluation carried out in 1994, 79.3 per cent saw the school experience as being most important in their course, and most associates report with great enthusiasm on their practical involvement, as for example where, 'I enjoyed my teaching practices with strong support from the mentor and the department'. The gains are clearly in areas like consistency of work, the more explicit links made between theory and practice, and in the area of integration with the work of the school. Yet despite the positive feelings about the process, there are nevertheless a number of areas which as yet remain problematic and there are reservations which reflect the training need. 'I felt that we could have had more guidance during the observation and final stages of the course when the mentors didn't seem to know what we were supposed to be doing...we lacked a clear idea'.

The roles of the different participants remain at times confused. This is often in relation to the changing expectations of the institutions involved. Thus how much input should be expected from the HEI and the nature of that input can often lead to misinterpretation and the potential for conflict. Importantly, this comes to a head when a weak associate, who often takes considerable time and energy from all those involved, needs a high degree of skill development, feedback and counselling. There is some evidence that weaker associates may have also sought more support from the staff of the HEI than they could give and that, because some mentors 'blamed the HEI for failure to support when they did not understand the changed way of working... the HEI tutor became the scapegoat'.

Another area of potential confusion relates to the monitoring process itself. Real partnership development requires that all those involved have a clear view of their own professional position. Yet it might well be argued that the role of the higher education institution remains a more senior one. Equally, it might well be argued that too much autonomy in the schools might give the system an inconsistency which professional mentors feel could have long-term detrimental effects on the associates. 'We really do need to have some sort of system which goes some way to give a common standard. It is difficult enough within the school but it becomes much more difficult when there are 30 involved. I suppose a new role of the HEI would be to give some accreditation for all this'.

## Higher Education Institution

Although often recently seen by the government as the major opponents of reform (see Chapter 1), the higher education institutions have been quick to recognize the value of the mentoring system. Yet in that recognition they have also needed to consider how they are to adapt to meet the new requirements of the changes. As indicated above, not only are new roles being required of those involved in the schools but also those in the HEI. Partnership requires recognition of three things. First, that the associates are not packages to be passed on after the inputs of the HEI, but they are developing through a strong integration of inputs from all those involved. In the current evaluation, 57.7 per cent of the associate respondents believed that this occurred most of the time. Second, the partners need to recognize that they do have both separate and common inputs to their work and in this there is evidence of success, with 75 per cent recognizing the contribution of the HEI to the course. Third, it needs to be recognized by all that they have a role in the integration of theory with practice and this is summed up in the comment of one associate who said that 'the course was an ideal blend of practice and theory', complemented by another associate who, in open comment, stated, 'I am concerned with the recent developments in education training that imply that the HEI is unimportant. It was a vital component, necessary for the course'.

The package role is clearly one that derives from the historical legacy of the old views of teaching practice. Often students arriving from college were either perceived by the schools as having inputs of theory, but relatively little practical knowledge, or had had expectations placed upon them which even the most helpful of HEIs could not deliver. In the development of mentoring, the partnership becomes all. Everyone involved needs to know what each is doing and each of the participants needs to know the parameters to their professional practice and judgement. In consequence, the role of the HEI tutor becomes much more that of a facilitator, able to promote or suggest relevant inputs themselves while allowing those in the schools to promote appropriate skills and roles. The difficulty arises when these roles are confused or when the resources available do not allow their full development. In curriculum terms we find the associate comment that 'the sort of maths we looked at with the staff in the HEI was different from that which the school was teaching and the clash of approaches led us to feel that we had been poorly lectured whilst doing the theoretical work'. In considering organization, another associate stated, 'there is so much work on differentiation within the schools and we need to know what the background to this is before we go for interview'. It must be said, however, that both these issues had been included in the documentation common to HEI and school courses and this raises the question of human infallibility, whatever the scheme put forward.

The need to develop different roles is clearly recognized by all. This is necessary if duplication and the underdevelopment of skills in the associates are to be avoided. Yet the promotion of those roles cannot be expected overnight. More importantly, the issues of common development and demarcation cannot be the sole responsibility of the HEI. This is illustrated in the school use of two periods of practice, induction and the final practice where associates are developing a range of skills through a pattern of involvement which may not involve traditional practice. Where 'the HEI staff had briefed the mentors and where the mentor had a good idea to use us for the development and evaluation of materials things were fine, but where we were doing time without a real pattern, things were awful'. Furthermore, it is important to realize that there are common inputs that need to be mutually reinforcing. All this leads to the conclusion that ongoing professional training for those involved is a must if the system is to fulfil its potential.

Within the developing role and changing world of teacher education, not only are the lines between HEIs and schools becoming blurred, but also that old distinction between theory and practice. A clear unintended consequence of the move to mentoring is that all those who recognize the need in future for professional reflexive practitioners in teaching do not maintain stereotypical views of the inputs made by those involved in the process. Greater communication through planning, increased mutual support, joint responsibility and shared values, about what constitutes good teaching, has broken for ever the easy prejudice that politicians have used to knock the teacher education world. Thus in the new roles taken on by the HEIs they are able to share some of the theory and relate it much more to the work in schools. Furthermore, clear inputs can be made by mentors as to the practical effects of the arguments. One associate commented that 'one of the best parts of the week was the weekly discussion with the professional mentor because it made what we had done either at college or in the classroom come alive'.

## Teacher Education and Training

As indicated previously, the complexity of what is happening cannot easily be dealt with by separating out the various elements that go to make up the world of mentoring and teacher education as it is developing. However, it is clear from the research we are promoting in this area, and despite numerous tensions and potential conflicts, that change is proceeding at a pace. Yet despite such insights, there is no doubt that the future, particularly for HEIs, remains somewhat uncertain. There is a clear role in the development of training and education approaches, in the piloting of materials and the fostering of research. It is also clear that many of the partner schools envisage an eventual role in some form of accreditation or quality control for participants in the scheme, but these moves, unless combined with a continuing partnership in teacher education, would inhibit the further development of good practice.

What therefore might be the implication of current developments in terms of the macro policy frameworks which were alluded to in Chapter 2? At a very simple level it might be concluded that despite the climate in which we work, HEIs and schools are developing partnerships which have clear and unambiguous potential for promoting a coherent framework for the development of teacher education. However, the challenges that are to come could place such developments in jeopardy unless government recognizes some of the implications now and some of the issues and problems alluded to.

It is clear that mentoring partnerships address many of the criticisms which have been thrown at teacher education in the past. Yet if they are to be successful, it is the partnerships which themselves need to be cultivated. There is no evidence that schools have any desire whatsoever to go it alone in the field of teacher education. Indeed, many would feel that too much emphasis on school consortia could effectively damage the good work that has so far been undertaken. It is vital therefore to see the nature of partnerships and the development of appropriate structures to facilitate their progress as central to a mentoring culture.

Equally important is the realization that the whole process needs to be carefully costed. Most of those involved, while currently giving enormous value for money, are also now beginning to count the costs to them or the school in both direct and indirect ways. There is no doubt that traditional teacher education, particularly the practice element, was on the cheap. Now, by beginning to celebrate the input made by schools, the whole system is becoming cost-conscious. While this cannot be measured purely in pounds, it is an issue which needs further investigation. The OFSTED emphasis on value for money in the school arena is being echoed in discussion concerning mentoring involvement: 'How can we talk about value for money when we look at the time taken to support associates and the pitiful transfer of fees to the schools – at some stage we have to doubt whether it is worthwhile being part of things' (headteacher). What can be said is that if we are to promote a coherent system, it is one that the competitive marketplace on its own will not easily deliver because the schools are not that eager to participate.

The development of professionalism, in all its forms, is also a vital element in the process. This will require concentration on two elements. First, the recognition by all that professionalism could be seen in the current world of corporate management styles as the catalyst that reasserts the value of the relatively autonomous classroom teacher. Fundamental to this will be the acceptance that mentoring is a vital ingredient that all teachers need to be involved in as they develop their own professional expertise. Second, this professionalism needs to be recognized more fully by the development of an accreditation framework which will support and enhance that professionalism. As a consequence, it is important that HEIs themselves need to incorporate that framework into their own development of partnerships. Our evidence is that this is beginning, and where it is developed it combines reflection on practice with understanding of the learning process and an opportunity for some extended investigation.

If there is a positive response to all of the above, then there might be some optimism for the future of mentoring partnerships. However, to suggest that politicians can be easily persuaded when particular ideological positions have been taken would be a little naive. Unless the evidence for mentoring partnerships is examined carefully and the process allowed to develop, we could be promoting a system where teachers become merely technical robots, trained but not educated. Real professional development needs to understand the complementary role of schools and HEIs in enhancing the profession of teaching. To sacrifice that development on the altar of political or economic expediency is to do a disservice to a pluralistic society and to ignore the future of many thousands of children to be taught by the teachers we educate and train.

# References

DfE (1992) *Initial Teacher Training (Secondary Phase)*, Circular 9/92 London: DfE.
*Times Educational Supplement*, Future of Teacher Education, News Item, 13.1.95.
Wilkin, M (1990) 'The Development of Partnership in the UK' in Booth, M, Furlong, J and Wilkin, M *Partnership in Initial Teacher Training*, London, Cassell.

# The Research Methodology

The purpose of the Keele University Department of Education investigations has been to ascertain the reality of the training experience and the policy impact of revised approaches to teacher education for the staff of the HEI concerned. The stakeholders have been identified as the subject and professional mentors within the schools, the other staff of schools who may not be directly involved in the training experience, and the pupils and the postgraduate associates who are at the heart of the changed arrangements.

Over the past five years the Centre for Successful Schools at Keele has been developing a particular approach to the collection of data from educational organizations. In general, this has included the use of a questionnaire, framed after a discussion with clients on the rationale for their own investigation, supported by individual interviews with up to 10 per cent of the cohort under investigation and an analysis of open, but anonymous, free comment invited from respondents at the conclusion of every questionnaire. This balance of qualitative and quantitative approaches has been followed in the compilation of this account of the investigation. The reports for the Post Graduate Certificate in Education (PGCE) Evaluation in 1993 and 1994 were separately commissioned, but have been used as additional material for this investigation.

After discussion with a team of five mentors of the possible contents of a mentor survey, a questionnaire to gauge mentors' perceptions of the organization, administration, philosophy and practice of the scheme was trialled and adapted in May 1994. The questionnaire was then sent to mentors in partnership schools in early July 1994. The professional mentors were asked to help with this by distributing the questionnaires, and collecting and posting them back to the department. We secured 101 responses, representing 64.3 per cent of the target group of 157 subject mentors. This was somewhat disappointing and leads us to ask whether the failure to respond is indicative of potentially negative comment or the pressures in schools at the end of a year.

The research of associate perceptions has been based on the use of questionnaires to all the PGCE associates at Keele in 1993 and 1994, together with 50 responses from associates at Worcester College of Higher Education in 1994. These additional responses were necessary to set some of the case studies into context. Collectively, this has given a database of experience and opinion from 500 teachers in training.

To supplement the questionnaires and the open comment which each respondent was invited to make, case study investigations were undertaken in 20 schools working within HEI partnerships at Keele University, Worcester College of Higher Education and St Martins College of Higher Education, Lancaster. The schools, and one college of further education, were selected to give a range of size (530–1,350 pupils); age range (11–16, 11–19); organization (including one grammar school and one college of further education); rural, suburban and inner-city location; previous involvement with the HEI concerned; previous educational history, and distance from the HEI with which they worked. Ten of these studies were conducted by one of the research team, but in the remaining ten schools the investigations were carried out by five practising mentors who each looked at the way in which the scheme worked within their own school and one other. To ensure consistency in approach and analysis, each study involved interviews with senior management staff, professional mentors, subject mentors, other staff and pupils. To maintain the focus on the way in which changed arrangements are creating a revised framework for initial teacher education and to identify the policy issues which are emerging, a semi-structured interview scheme was used. This was based upon a sequence which considered the impact of change upon schools, the evolution of policy and practice for the personnel involved, and the issues arising from changed expectations of role within the partnership. The main areas for investigation were:

a. *The Institutional Framework*
   Changes in institutional structures
   The management of change
   Resource distribution
   Time management
   Processes of mentoring
   Implications for school and pupils

b. *Individual Relationships*
   Mentor selection
   Role definition and negotiation
   Career profile and expectations
   Skill identification and development
   Personal training and development needs
   Mentor motivation

c. *Consequences*
   Control of the system
   Benefits and tensions
   Partnership issues
   Quality evaluation and maintenance
   Value for money
   Research and evaluation

Discussions of these issues were recorded as field notes and these were incorporated into the 20 case study reports which were then collated and analysed to provide a single qualitative report. This was subsequently linked with quantitive data from questionnaire evidence to provide the basis for consideration of the issues in this book. Discussion of the total evidence led to the proposition that there is a conceptual 'mentoring environment' which affects both the training experience and the potential for the achievement of successful outcomes and, while we have been concerned with the identification and impact of major policy issues as they affect schools, we have also looked at the internal and external environmental elements of the changed practice.

# Index